D0948523

Accept the Challenge:
The Memoirs of Jerry Clinton

by Jerry Clinton

*with Rob Rains
and a Foreword by Dan Dierdorf*

Library of Congress Cataloging-in-Publication Data: on file

ISBN-13: 978-1-933370-01-9
ISBN-10: 1-933370-01-7

Published in cooperation with
Reedy Press
PO Box 5131, St. Louis, MO 63139, USA

For all information on all Reedy Press publications visit our website at
www.reedypress.com.

Printed in the United States of America
06 07 08 09 10   5 4 3 2 1

Text design by Matthew Heidenry
and Risto Kekich
Cover design by Bruce Burton

This book is dedicated to my grandsons Mark, Nathan, Riley, Myles, and Cole Clinton.

My generation didn't leave you a perfect world . . . far from it! Keep your faith in God and maintain high ethical standards, and you could go far in providing respect for our democracy, improving our ecology, and promoting world peace.

I love you all!

I would also like to give special thanks to Jolie and Alan Zvibleman for their advice and friendship.

Contents

Foreword

YOU DO NOT MEET MANY people in your life like Jerry Clinton. I have been fortunate to be a personal friend of Jerry's for more than thirty years, and he is the type of man who doesn't ask for anything and gives everything. If you tried to put all of the items and contributions that Jerry Clinton has donated to charities over the years into a room you probably would fill up the Edward Jones Dome.

Jerry's story is really a wonderful illustration of the opportunities that we all have in this great country of ours. You can start with nothing, and through hard work and dedication you can hit it big. Jerry is the embodiment of that. It is a concept and principle that our country is based on.

One of Jerry's biggest attributes is that success did not change him. He has never been anything other than a Golden Gloves boxer. Jerry has always been fighting for whatever cause he thought was worth pursuing.

Jerry knows that you don't win every fight. His story illustrates that you don't accomplish everything in life that you set out to accomplish. I was a believer at the time and still believe that it was because of Jerry Clinton's efforts that the domed stadium was built in St. Louis. Jerry was the man who got behind the steering wheel and agreed to try to make it happen.

Jerry did not reach his goal of acquiring an expansion franchise in the NFL for St. Louis. If he had been a billionaire it would have been a lot easier to make that happen. He didn't get the ball across the goal line, but he was the one who put together a long series of first downs to get the winning drive started. Whether you agree or disagree with his tactics, nobody can deny that he was the one who got the drive started to bring the NFL back to St. Louis.

We have enjoyed so many great moments together over the years. When I was inducted into the Pro Football Hall of Fame in 1996, Jerry rented out a restaurant after the ceremony and we had a private party for about 200 people. Jerry paid for the entire event as his gift to me.

Another moment I will never forget was when we attempted to take a picture of our slow-pitch softball team at Grant's Farm, standing next to one of the bison. Our team name was the Bison, and it might have been one of the dumbest things I have ever attempted in my life. For some reason I honestly believed we could just walk up there and put our arm around this thing and he would stand there and let us take a picture.

You don't realize from seeing them on television how unbelievably big these animals are. We got off Jerry's motor coach, and it was about fifty feet away from us. It looked at me, and I looked at him. I was a strapping young man then, and I was scared to death. It was my idea and Jerry went along with it, but it was a bad idea. We were lucky to get out of there unharmed.

Jerry has had the privilege of meeting and becoming friends with many famous people in his life, among them actor and racecar driver Paul Newman and the late Walter Payton. We also shared a mutual friendship with Jack Buck. In my world, if Jack Buck was your friend there was no need to run a personality check or a criminal investigation. There was no need for you to know anything else other than that Jack Buck says you are his friend. That's really almost the only epitaph you would need on your tombstone: "Here lies Dan Dierdorf or Jerry Clinton . . . He was Jack Buck's friend."

Jerry also has a lot of friends who are not famous or well known. He has been a friend and supporter of almost every charitable cause in the St. Louis region for the past forty years, and many of the people served by those charities have had their lives brightened by the efforts of Jerry Clinton. They might never have met him or had the opportunity to say thank you, but Jerry was there to help them in their time of need. There is probably not a family of the employees of Grey Eagle that has not been touched by his efforts in some way.

All of Jerry's friends got a chance to show how much he means to them on the tragic day when his son Jeff was killed in a car racing accident. We formed a protective cocoon around him and let him know we were there for him.

That tragedy also revealed Jerry's strength. He didn't curl up and die. He had grandkids to take care of and a business to run, and he did both with the same drive and determination he has maintained his entire life.

Jerry has done so many things for so many people that you almost have to tell him to stop, but he never will. He doesn't know the meaning of the word. You can always count on Jerry, and he never asks for anything. That makes him a very special man, and someone I am honored to call my friend.

Dan Dierdorf
October 2006

Preface

THE LATE DUNCAN BAUMAN, PUBLISHER of the now-defunct *St. Louis Globe-Democrat*, said to me once, "Jerry, you have to write a book."

"Why do you say that Duncan?" I asked.

"Because what you have done with building the domed stadium is part of St. Louis history, and it needs to be recorded properly and God knows it has not been by our local newspaper," he said.

I guess those were the words that inspired me to write this book. It was more than the stadium, however. Young aspiring people frequently ask me, "How did you achieve your success?" Thinking about that question prompted me to reflect on my life and the contributions I have been able to make to my family, employees, and community. Even more importantly, I realized writing a book would give me the opportunity to give my grandsons a piece of their family history through my activities, and also share these events with our community. It also reflects how our country and its opportunities have changed over time, especially since the Great Depression.

If you find anything in these pages that is informative or in some way inspiring, then I know my effort will have been worthwhile.

I love the St. Louis community, even with its faults and its layers of diverse society. It rolls along like our great Mississippi River in normal times, but when its banks get flooded, we come together for the greater good. We build a domed stadium with even greater economic benefits for all as a result of a message from a beer salesman who cares. It is what it is . . . and so it is.

I hope you enjoy my story.

Jerry Clinton
October 2006

Prologue

AS I HAVE HAD THE opportunity to reflect back on my life, one of the conclusions I have reached is that I, in particular, am a product of my environment. I have realized how hard work has played a major role in shaping the outcome of my life, but I also realize how lucky I have been along the way.

There have been numerous events that happened along my life's journey that have affected and influenced my life, both positively and negatively. These events affected my personality and my way of thinking. They literally changed my life.

Much of my childhood was spent growing up in the housing projects in St. Louis, where tragedy was almost a daily event. I learned the lesson at a young age about how delicate life can be.

I learned that there are specific rules in society. If you break these rules you are going to find yourself in a very unhappy environment. If you work hard enough, live by the rules, and get enough lucky breaks along the way, your life can be very successful and rewarding.

That is what happened to me. I want to share my life's journey, because I think it offers lessons that have not only affected my life but also affected the lives of many other people, some of whom I have never even met.

This book is the story of a large segment of my life, the stories of the people I met along the way, and the stories of the significant events that have occurred over the past sixty-plus years. There will be much additional detail in the pages that follow, but I wanted to share some of the highlights with you.

I was born in a house that had no electricity or indoor plumbing, and spent much of my childhood living in the housing projects. Stan Musial was my boyhood hero, as he was to thousands of other young boys growing up in St. Louis in the 1940s and 1950s. Who knew he would later become a trusted friend and business partner.

At that point in my life, it seemed ridiculous to think I would grow up to own a multimillion-dollar company, one of the leading wholesalers in the Anheuser-Busch beer empire. I never thought I would become a professional racecar driver.

Little did I know or even imagine that only a few miles from where I grew up, a gleaming domed stadium would now stand, home to an NFL franchise. I truly believe that if I had not led the campaign through the various legislative bodies, then that stadium would never have been built and the Rams would be playing in some other city. I am proud of that.

I will forever be grateful that I was able to become good friends with people such as Jack Buck and Dan Dierdorf. I enjoyed my friendships with Paul Newman and Walter Payton. We lost Walter too early when he died in 1999 at the age of forty-five from liver disease. Had our ownership group been successful in landing an expansion NFL franchise for St. Louis, Walter would have been our general manager and league representative as well as the first black owner of an NFL franchise. I know he would have done a great job. I will have much more to say about all of these men later in this book.

People often think that not getting that team was a major disappointment for me, and it was. In reality, however, we accomplished what our group set out to do. We got a new stadium built, which has produced a great economic impact for the city beyond football, and we helped bring the NFL back to St. Louis. I do take pride in knowing I played a role in making that happen.

I have had the good fortune of helping raise a lot of money for charitable causes, especially the Backstoppers and Marygrove Center, a facility for abused children in Florissant. Knowing you have helped, even in a small way, improve the lives of people who are suffering is a wonderful feeling.

The greatest pain I have endured in my life was the death of my son, Jeff, in a motor sport racing accident in 2002. I wept each day for forty days after Jeff died. It was a tragedy in every sense of the word. Jeff was a great son, a great father, a great businessman, and a wonderful friend. I miss him everyday and so do a lot of other family members and friends.

It was the love of family and friends that allowed me to stay strong during this time in my life, and I am eternally grateful for their support. Certainly at the top of the list is Terri Larkin. Terri is a wonderful companion that I had known and had grown to love for five years preceding this tragic event. She had even gained the respect and friendship of Jeff, which she richly deserved. She was always there for me during the dark days following his death.

Terri lost her father when she was only six years old and therefore helped me understand the feelings of my grandsons, Mark and Nathan, in dealing with their loss. I truly don't know how I could have survived without her love and support. I also need to express my love and support to my son Brian and his wife Megan, in addition to Jo, the mother of my two sons. We all rejoiced as our family grew, and we suffered our greatest loss together.

I realize that life isn't meant to be fair, and none of us know how much time we have left. For each and every one of us, our goal in life should be to accept the challenge of whatever tasks come before us, both personally and professionally.

When I look back on my life, I really think these three words form a perfect summation—Accept the Challenge. Challenges are exactly that, and they come in every size, shape, and form imaginable, big and small. How you deal with those challenges affects every other aspect of your life.

Every time I was faced with a challenge, and accepted it, the outcome played a major role in my future. Likewise, if I had refused to accept a challenge, who knows how my life would have turned out?

What if I had decided not to apply for a job at Anheuser-Busch when I was eighteen years old? What if I hadn't been willing to accept different jobs at the brewery, moving through various offices, allowing me to meet and get to know different people?

What if I had decided to stay at Anheuser-Busch instead of going to a new company, Grey Eagle? What if I had decided to leave Anheuser-Busch to start selling life insurance?

Many times during my career at Grey Eagle I was faced with challenging business decisions. We had a terrible strike in 1976 that affected the future of the company. What if I had not accepted Tom Burrows' challenge to become the sales manager and had not stayed up all night preparing a sales budget? I think I know the answer to that question: I never would have become the president and later the owner of the company.

Did I make some bad choices in my life? Absolutely. Are there some decisions I would like to do over again? Certainly.

In the larger picture of life, however, I know I've been blessed, and I would be the first person to acknowledge that. By the same token, however, I do think a person has a lot to do with making his own luck by working hard, dedicating himself to a project or cause, and not being satisfied until the job is done. Good things don't just happen by accident all the time.

I really think that is how I have tried to live my life. Looking back, I don't really think there is anything I would have done or could have done differently. Thank you for going on this journey with me.

Chapter 1

THE MOVIE *CINDERELLA MAN* BROUGHT a tear to my eye when the main character, boxer James J. Braddock, took food off his breakfast plate and gave it to his daughter, who had eaten but was still hungry. He said he was full and didn't want his food, even though he had not taken one bite.

I wondered how many times my father had done the same thing when my sister, three brothers, and I were young.

We grew up in the Great Depression, and as anybody from my generation knows, those were extremely difficult times. I am sure there were many times my father, Harry Clinton, went to bed at night without having as much as a quarter in his pocket with seven mouths to feed. That was a mark of real character, to hustle and find a job so you could feed your family. A lot of fathers abandoned their families during those years. My father did not. He was not the heavyweight champion of the world, but he was a champion in my book.

Because my father could not find work in St. Louis and was too proud to stand in a bread line, he moved his family to the tiny town of Graniteville, Missouri, about eighty-five miles south of St. Louis near what is now the Elephant Rocks State Park. At one time there was a thriving granite quarry there. My grandfather and other relatives had worked at the quarry. One day when my father was a small boy, my grandfather was working on a crane, and my dad's brother volunteered to go under the crane to adjust a harness before they lifted the huge block of granite. The crane shifted for some reason, and my uncle was killed.

By the time the Depression hit, the quarry was pretty much

shut down because of a lack of orders. My paternal grand-mother still owned a small piece of land in town, and there was a small frame house consisting of about two-and-a-half rooms. It had no electricity and no plumbing. I was born there on a stormy April morning in 1937.

There were holes in the roof, and when it rained, my mother, Thelma, had to put pans and buckets around the house to catch all the leaks. We heated the home in the winter with a pot-belly, wood-burning stove. When the fire went out at night the water would freeze in the water bucket, and in the morning you would have to break up the ice so you could start priming the pump at the kitchen sink. We had coal oil lamps, but we went to bed pretty early in the evening because we couldn't afford to keep them lit very long. My two brothers and I slept in one bed, my older brother was on a cot in our room, and my sister slept on a cot in my parents' room.

We never knew we were that poor, which again is a tribute to my parents. We weren't any different than anybody else—if there was no work, there was no money. If there was no money, there was not enough food.

My parents grew vegetables during the summer so we would have something to eat in the winter. My dad got a job through the WPA, set up by President Roosevelt, shoveling sand out of river bottoms. He made maybe a dollar a day.

The quarry operated a small store and the post office in town, where they let people charge food and other items. It seemed we always had a small bill at the "company store." Whenever my dad had money, he went to the store and paid what he could on his bill. My younger brother Bill and I often went with him, and Mae Sheahan, who owned and operated the store, would give my dad five round "jawbreakers," one for each of his kids, in a small, brown paper bag. It was the only candy we ever had. We popped the jawbreaker in our mouths and took a few licks before we took it out so we could save part of it for the next day.

One Christmas my sister Betty took charge and had us all write letters to Santa. We put them in the stove, thinking that the ashes would carry to the North Pole, where Santa would somehow be able to read them. Christmas was always pretty lean in those years. My dad would go out and cut down a cedar tree, and my sister would cut contact paper into strips and make paste out of flour and water. She used the strips to decorate the tree. We cut out a star from the paper and put it on top of the tree.

When I was four years old, we woke up on Christmas morning, and there was nothing under the tree. My dad said he didn't know if Santa was going to be able to make it that year, because we lived in such a remote area and there was no snow! Later that afternoon my father's cousin and his wife who lived in St. Louis showed up. They had a present for each of us, some fruit, and a little Mickey Mouse acrobat toy. That was our Christmas, and the "Santa story" was saved for another year.

My mother got a job working at the Brown Shoe Co. factory in Arcadia, Missouri, and they would sell seconds to the employees at a very reduced price. She bought me a pair, and I didn't want to wear them because I was afraid I would ruin them. Most of my clothes were the third set of hand-me-downs. By the time I got them they were pretty well shot, so I didn't know what it was like to wear something new.

When World War II broke out, my dad was able to get a job working at a defense plant in St. Louis. We stayed in Graniteville, and he commuted on the weekends. It was hard for me to see him leave every Sunday night, because I wanted him to be there with me. But it was a job, and before long he had earned enough money that he was able to move the entire family to St. Louis.

We moved to a two-room flat on Lafayette Avenue near Lafayette Park in south St. Louis. Several families shared one bathroom in the main hallway, but it was still a better home than we had known. When my dad left the defense plant to go to work for the Midwest Pipe and Supply Co., which later became the

Crane Corp., we moved again, this time into an apartment in the Clinton-Peabody Housing Project.

Life was still tough, as it was for many low-income families, but we had five well-heated rooms. We walked to the Clinton-Peabody grade school, and we also would go home for lunch. The school served a hot lunch, but it cost ten cents. Most of the time we didn't have the ten cents, because with four kids in school that added up pretty quickly, and money was still tight. We would leave school smelling the meatloaf or other food cooking in the cafeteria, then go home and eat a sandwich and drink a glass of milk for lunch. Some days, there was no lunchmeat or cheese, so we would just eat the bread, then go back to school.

My oldest brother Harry Jr. had quit high school and went to work. Like most young working people of that time, he paid weekly board money into the family budget.

As I grew older, I began to realize more about our family's economics. We received free dental care in the basement of the Malcolm Bliss Mental Hospital, but when the dentist had to drill, he didn't use Novocain. It was a frightening experience.

My father was a big baseball fan, as was my grandfather. My uncle Mike had been a catcher in the Browns' minor-league organization. My grandfather was a catcher in amateur baseball growing up in southeast Missouri, and he didn't have one straight finger on either hand. They didn't use gloves in those days, catching the ball barehanded.

We played on an asphalt parking lot at school, and we didn't have the best of equipment. We wrapped a baseball in electrical tape so it would last longer. One day at recess, one of the bigger kids in the school was at the plate with a bat with a knob chipped off from hitting the asphalt too many times. As he swung and hit the ball, the bat flew out of his hands and hit the boy who was on deck, Tommy Parker, right in the forehead. Even though the school was next door to City Hospital, Tommy was dead by the time he got there.

We listened to the Cardinals' games on the radio, and I had pictures of Stan Musial and Red Schoendienst on the walls of my bedroom. Stan was everybody's hero, and I liked Red because I played second base, as he did. I wasn't much of a hitter, but I could cover a lot of ground and was a pretty good fielder. Some friends I made in those days remain friends today, including Bobby Sansone—the first baseman on our team and a future St. Louis Teamster leader.

Our team was sponsored by local merchants, so each kid wore the name of a different sponsor. I was one of the smallest kids on the team, and my sponsor happened to be Flotkin's 39th Street Supermarket. My uniform shirt couldn't have said Joe's Market or something short. Half of the name was tucked into my uniform pants.

We took the streetcar up to Sportsman's Park to see a game one time, and I was close enough to Stan that I could have asked for his autograph, but I was too shy and didn't want to bother him, because he was with his son. Years later I got the autograph.

I also was a big boxing fan as a boy, with heroes such as Joe Louis, Rocky Marciano, and Sugar Ray Robinson. Louis had a big fight one time, and it was broadcast on the radio. My dad let me stay up late to listen to it. Joe won and I was thrilled. Later we got our first television, a twelve-inch black and white Philco, and I always wanted to make sure I was home on Wednesday and Friday nights so I could watch the 9 p.m. fights.

My father got a raise at work, but it wasn't entirely good news. He now was earning two dollars a week more than one could make and still live in a government housing project. We were forced to leave our home on Castle Lane and go back to the "cold water flats" several blocks east, at the corner of 10th and Rutger Streets.

In those days, there were a lot of rough kids in that neighborhood, and they would get in trouble from time to time. I hung out with them because I considered them friends, but I knew they were getting involved in activities that weren't right. They would steal things from stores, then give them to a bread truck driver, who would fence the items for them. They got into a lot of fights on the street but didn't get anything out of them, other than a knot on the head. I knew the South Broadway Athletic Club had a great reputation for turning out boxing champions. There, if you won a fight, you got a medal. I decided I would rather have a medal than a knot on the head. I left the street corner and spent my evenings training at the South Broadway A.C.

The Clinton boys always stuck together, and people soon realized if there was trouble in the neighborhood, we were going to meet it head-on. You might be able to beat me, but not my brother. My father always said for us not to start a fight but, if we got into one for some reason, to make damn sure that we finished it. We always accepted the challenge.

My oldest brother Harry Jr. was a boxer, as was my future brother-in-law, Al Freeman. They fought out of the downtown YMCA. Boxing was big then. I met the coach of South Broadway, Joe Weber, but he didn't have much time for me. He had about fifty or sixty boxers he was getting ready for the Golden Gloves competition. When Joe finally realized I wasn't going anywhere, he took more of an interest in me and worked to develop my skills. He spent one entire Sunday afternoon teaching me how to throw a left hook.

My younger brother, Bill, and I both entered the Golden Gloves the same year. He won the championship boxing for the Boys Club of St. Louis. I lost my second fight. I had to wait a whole year to redeem myself, looking at his medal hanging on the bedroom wall, and that made me more determined than ever to become a better fighter. The next year I won the championship and earned my own medal. My brother Russ tried boxing for a while, but his Rudolph Valentino nose, he thought, was worth preserving.

Boxing was a sport I really enjoyed, because I think it matched my interest in competition and in relying on myself to be success-ful. You didn't need to have somebody tell you when you made a mistake in the ring; you realized it immediately. It was up to you to figure out how to keep it from happening again.

The first time my name was ever in the newspaper was when they listed the pairings for the Golden Gloves fights, and it was exciting. I was mentioned in a couple of write-ups as "the smooth working fighter from South Broadway" who should do well. I also won a regional AAU championship, and we were paid a few bucks to fight exhibitions at country clubs while members had drinks and dinner. We were usually fed but in the kitchen.

My mother and father came to all of my fights, and my mother was my biggest fan. I could always hear her yelling, no matter how much noise the rest of the crowd was making. She was always offering me great advice like "Come on Jerry, kill him," or something to that effect. She was a tough little cookie. There were always rules in the projects for things such as when your wash day was and how many clothes lines you could use. If somebody took one of her lines, she was perfectly willing to tell them in her special way! She was spunky, while my dad was more laid back and reserved.

Once, I was on the fight card at the American Legion Hall in Wellston, Missouri, and when the fights were over my dad told me to get in the front seat of our car, a 1942 Plymouth, so we could talk about my fight. We were on the way home when we were hit head-on by a panel truck that had been stolen by some kids out for a joy ride. My father broke his back and my mom had a fractured skull. I hit the windshield but luckily just had a bunch of cuts and bruises. The next day, I had a lot of explain-ing to do—to tell people I had been in a car wreck on the way home and that I had not gotten beat up in the fight.

Getting off the street corner and into more organized box-ing was one of the best moves I made as a youngster, because if I had continued to hang around with that gang, I would have found myself in trouble. One friend I hung out with was Sonny Faheen. We used to ride bikes and play baseball together. Years later he was killed in a car bombing at the Mansion House. I graduated from school with Joe Broderick, and he was later implicated in the car-bombing death of Jimmy Michaels. I knew Paul Leisure. He also was reportedly involved in some underworld activities and was later car-bombed. He eventually died in prison. That was the type of neighborhood I lived in growing up.

My brother Russ got a job working at the Terrace Delicatessen on Chouteau Avenue, between 14th and 18th Streets. When he got older and took a better job, I went to work there. It sold everything from beer to ice cream to canned goods, and I would work there after school in the winter and all day in the summer, sometimes twelve to fourteen hours a day, making thirty-five to fifty cents an hour. I mopped the floors, worked the counter, cleaned, burned the trash, did whatever needed to be done. The deli was next door to the Tradewinds Bar, which was owned by the Faheen family.

I was working one evening when a boy I knew from school stopped and waved as he got ready to cross Chouteau Avenue on his way to the movies. I waved back, and as he turned to cross the street, he apparently misjudged how fast an eighteen-wheeler was going by and walked right into the rear wheels. He had just been waving at me, and thirty seconds later he was lying on the street, dead. It was pretty shocking.

I remember another time a small girl was struck and killed by a cement mixer. The projects were surrounded by truck routes, ambulance lanes, etc. Those kinds of accidents happened all the time when I was a kid.

My other part-time job when I was in school was working as a pinsetter at the bowling alley. It was hard work. You would work for six hours setting the pins, and if your were lucky at the end of the night—if you had done a good job—the bowlers would slide some money down the gutter toward you. Most of the money you made came from tips. You had to be careful to get out of the way of the flying pins, because those things really hurt when they cracked you on the shin. I would make four or five dollars on a good night, which I thought was good money.

After graduating from the eighth grade at Clinton-Peabody School, I went to Hadley Tech, a vocational high school that became Vashon High School after I graduated in 1955. I was not a big fan of school and was mostly a C student. However, I still remember some of my teachers and, thinking about it now, realize they had more influence on me and my future than I realized during my time at Clinton-Peabody. Marie Schicker was a great woman and took a profound interest in the kids that she taught. Regina O'Neill was a very bright woman and really stressed the importance of good values.

My younger brother Bill and I had our first chance to escape the neighborhood when my uncle invited us to spend a couple of summers with his family at their home in Denver and at a little cabin they owned in the mountains near Wyoming. E. Michael "Mickey" Clinton had started out as a truck driver and had moved up to become a vice president of the company, the Ringsby truck line. Once, he bought us a Continental Airline ticket and sent us home on a twin-engine propeller flight, my first time ever on an airplane. It was a pretty bumpy ride, and Bill and I sat there gripping the seats and staring at each other wondering if we were ever going to make it back to the street corner.

My older brothers had all dropped out of high school before they graduated, but I finished and graduated in 1955. I was really disappointed my younger brother Bill dropped out the same year I graduated, when he was a sophomore. They all wanted to go to work and start making money. I tried to lecture Bill that he was making a mistake, but families didn't emphasize getting an education the way they do today, so there were a lot of dropouts in that era.

We were a blue-collar union family, like many folks, and the idea in that day was to hook up with a labor union to get some job security and decent health and retirement benefits. My father was a union man, and all my brothers became union workers. They eventually worked themselves into supervisory or management positions. My father encouraged me to do that too.

I spent a lot of time visiting with my grandparents while I was in high school, running errands for them. One morning my grandmother got up to fix my grandfather his breakfast. He had fallen and broken his hip and had just been sent home from City Hospital. My grandmother had long hair, down past her waist, which she usually wore up on top of her head, but she took it down at night when she went to bed. Since she had just gotten up, it was still down.

She turned on the gas at the kitchen stove, but it didn't ignite. The pilot light had gone out, but she didn't smell any gas. She struck a match to light it, and the whole kitchen exploded. She was burned very badly and lost all of her beautiful hair. She lived six days in the hospital before she died. My father refused to let me visit her in the hospital because he wanted me to remember her as she was.

When I was a senior in high school, the school helped you get a vocation-related job where you worked half of the day, then went to school the rest of the day. I was hired at a process letter company at 22nd and Locust, the Charles B. Wilkes Co. Even though I loved the people there, I didn't care much for the job. Mostly, I ran a lot of errands. The company's biggest client was *The Sporting News,* whose office at the time was on Washington Avenue. It was through that job that I met a lot of the people there, including the publisher, J. G. Taylor Spink.

The company hired me full time after high school, and even though I didn't care much for the work I was doing, I was glad to have a job. I had to ride a city bus part of the way to work, then switch to the Jefferson Avenue streetcar. One morning I was standing at the bus stop, in the rain, with my paper sack lunch tucked under my arm when a car pulled up. The guys in the car asked if I needed a ride.

I said yes so I could get out of the rain, and they asked where I was going. It turned out the driver was a young man named Don Sorich, and he worked in the same building as I did. His employer occupied the fourth floor, one floor below me. We both worked there about a year, when I found out he was leaving to go to work for Anheuser-Busch. He encouraged me to apply there, and I did.

When I didn't hear anything from the brewery, I took a job with the Grace Sign Co. In my mind, it was a definite sweatshop. The job had nothing to do with commercial art, which I had studied in high school. It was about making signs and painting and embossing them. People were consistently getting their fingers cut off in the presses. I hated the job and couldn't wait to find something else.

Going through the mail one day after work I discovered a letter from Anheuser-Busch. They had reviewed my application and had a "position" open that they thought I might be qualified for. Would I be available to come down for an interview? I was really surprised because it had been about a year since I had filled out the application. I didn't know they kept the applications on file that long.

Excited, I went to the interview and was thrilled when I got the job. I was assigned to the office services department, which basically meant that we supplied all of the offices at Anheuser-Busch with their office-product needs, from furniture to paper clips.

At the time, I was glad to have a job that I enjoyed and really had no long-term career goals. That was soon going to change.

Chapter **2**

AT THE AGE OF NINETEEN, I was just happy to have a steady job at a good company. I really was not thinking about life beyond the immediate future.

Delivering office supplies provided a variety of assignments, and one of my duties was to make deliveries to both August A. Busch Jr.'s private railroad car and to his office at Sportsman's Park.

Mr. Busch did not like airplanes, and he traveled around the country as much as possible on his private railroad car. It was my job to drop off items that he needed, such as magazines—I think *Field and Stream* was his favorite—toothpaste, and grooming items before he went out of town.

During the baseball season, I had to make a daily run to Sportsman's Park, driving a 1955 Chevrolet Budweiser station wagon, to take the same type of items to his suite at the ballpark. I also had to pick up tickets for the game that day that had been ordered by Anheuser-Busch employees and bring them back to the brewery.

One day I met Mr. Busch while he was in his office. He was a very gruff-talking man, and I don't think I was the only person who was a little intimidated and scared the first time I walked into his office. But I was to find out over the next several years that he actually was a very friendly man once you got to know him and was approachable. We were able to build a nice relationship, which was meaningful and important to me.

I also met one of my boyhood idols, Stan Musial. One of his children was getting married, and he needed a new CO_2 tank for his home draught beer system. Late one afternoon somebody came down to the delivery office and asked if anyone could take it to his house. I volunteered, and I will never forget the two of us working to get the tank hooked up while Stan's wife Lil was yelling at him to hurry up because their guests would be there any minute.

Guess who else I soon ran into in my new job? My old friend Don Sorich, who had tipped me off about working for Anheuser-Busch. Don was in the office that ordered the supplies we stocked for the brewery's various departments. We renewed our friendship, and he eventually sold me my first car, a 1949 Oldsmobile '88.

I was becoming more serious about my future. I transferred to some different departments within Anheuser-Busch, and I took some night classes at Washington University.

Without a college education, even back then, I knew my future likely would have to be in some department such as sales, where your success or failure is determined more by how you interact and relate with people than by how many degrees you have. I transferred to the design section of the engineering department at the brewery and met some smart and interesting people.

Even though I was several years younger than everybody else who worked there, these guys took me under their wing and really influenced my life. What they really did was teach me how to think. Engineers and architects are very logical people, because they think out everything. These guys were interested in issues beyond work, and we had great discussions during breaks and lunch about politics, the arts, music, everything. I just tried to listen to them as much as possible and soak up as much knowledge as they were willing to give.

They included me in all of their activities, including a three-day float trip down the Meramec River, dinner dances, and other social activities. We remained friends, even after I moved on, and I don't think they had any idea how much they taught me. Harold Greenblatt, Charles Bieger, and John Oefelien are some that I kept in touch with for many years.

In 1958, a letter arrived in the mail one day from another entity interested in my services—the U.S. Army. I had been drafted. In those days, after you completed your basic training assignment, you had the choice of splitting your time between active duty and the reserves, or going into what they called the "ready reserves." That meant your unit would be one of the first ones activated should the need arise. Either way, you had to make a six-year commitment to the army.

I chose the "ready reserves" since it seemed to make more sense. After your active duty service, you were allowed to work at your civilian job, but if the army decided they needed you, you had to go grab a rifle and do your thing. There were a lot of little flare-ups over the next couple of years, and I thought I might be going somewhere, but luckily the situations were resolved before we reached that point.

That letter finally arrived in 1961, when I was ordered again to report to active duty. I was told to clean up my personal affairs and be ready to report on twenty-four-hours notice. American and Russian tanks were staring each other down in Berlin. I had previously met my future wife Jo while I was at training in Wisconsin. She had moved to St. Louis and had gotten a job as a hair stylist, and we were planning to be married. We didn't know what to do, because we didn't know if I would be headed to Germany or somewhere else, and we didn't know when.

I sold my car and got everything ready, but I just waited. Maybe the Russians heard I was coming and backed off. Finally, about four months later, I received another letter that told me the previous orders had been rescinded and that I was being returned to ready-reserve status. It was now time to continue my life.

I knew my future at Anheuser-Busch was not going to be in the engineering department because of my lack of architecture and drafting background, so when an opening came up in the insurance department, I transferred there. It seemed like a good idea at the time, and was basically the type of sales job I thought would be the right fit, but I soon discovered that I was not fond of the insurance business.

My job basically was to determine the value of claims and to do a lot of the clerical work. I had to decide how much insurance we needed in certain areas of the brewery. What I really decided, however, was that the basic concept of an insurance company is to force you to bet against yourself. They want you to prepare as if some disaster is going to happen, and this went against my way of thinking. I prefer to be a positive individual.

Still, despite my objections to the insurance business, I received a job offer from the General American Insurance Co. and was seriously considering it. I thought it would be a sales job and that if I got more into the nuts and bolts of the process, I might develop a different attitude.

Before I agreed to take the job, however, I received a call from the Anheuser-Busch personnel department telling me about a job opening in the delivery section of the city sales department. Even though the job wasn't in sales, I thought that working in the department would help my opportunity for a transfer if a sales job opened up. This turned out to be a major break for me, because I know that if I had accepted the job with General American I would not have been happy and soon would have been looking for another job somewhere else. I concluded that it was better to take a job that paid less with a better potential for the future than to take more money with less future potential.

During those years, local beer sales and distribution was different than it is today. The brewery operated its own sales branch, which sold and delivered the product in the City of St. Louis and in St. Louis County, basically operating as its own distribution company. My first job was at the city delivery office at the corner of Broadway and Arsenal, dispatching truck drivers. I had to check them in and out, making certain their sales orders and deliveries and returns balanced. I worked long hours but learned a great deal about that part of the brewery's operation, including an inflationary labor contract.

In 1962, Anheuser-Busch made the decision that it would create an independent wholesaler to handle distribution of its beer in St. Louis County. Thomas Burrows, who had been the vice president and national sales manager at the time, talked August Busch Jr. into giving him the opportunity, as he preferred to settle in St. Louis rather than travel around the country. Burrows would need people to staff the new company, so he came to our office to conduct interviews. I was one of those selected to work for the new company.

When he offered me a job, it really was not a hard decision. I would still be doing something I knew how to do, and enjoyed, and doing it for a company with fewer layers of management than existed at a large corporation such as Anheuser-Busch. I had been at Anheuser-Busch seven years, but I knew I could work my tail off and spend my entire career there unnoticed by senior management because of the multiple layers of middle management.

I accepted the job, knowing that if I was worth anything, Tom Burrows was going to know it. This became a life-altering event for me. Once again I was happy to accept the challenge.

Chapter 3

I DIDN'T EVEN KNOW WHAT the name of the new company was going to be. Neither did Tom Burrows, until he met with Mr. Busch one day.

Mr. Busch for years had been known as the "Big Eagle." Tom had prematurely gray hair; he had a full head of gray hair when he was thirty years old. Consequently, Mr. Busch referred to him as his "Grey Eagle." At their meeting, Mr. Busch asked Tom what he was going to name the new company.

"I really don't have any idea," Tom said. "I haven't even thought about it."

"I've got a name for you," Mr. Busch said. "Grey Eagle Distributors."

Tom told me later he shook his head and replied, "Boss, I think you just named the company."

Grey Eagle opened on May 1, 1963, with twenty-two salaried employees and about forty-five drivers. My job was much the same as it had been in my last assignment at the brewery, dispatching trucks and drivers and tracking their sales and deliveries. My salary was $125 a week. We worked out of a temporary office, the Motor Transportation Company warehouse on Gratiot St. This company leased our trucks to us in the early years. The warehouse was hot and dirty. We had beer stacked everywhere, and it was almost impossible to take a decent inventory.

One of my jobs was to determine how much beer we needed and order it three weeks in advance of shipping. Our drivers were accustomed to receiving a lot of overtime when they worked for Anheuser-Busch. They were coming back to the office late, and often I would not leave work until 10 p.m. Jo was expecting our first child, and I left her home an inordinate amount of time working hard to get my job done. I attempted to stay up late when I got home so we could have some time together, but then I would have to get up early and work another twelve-to-fourteen-hour day.

At the time, Anheuser-Busch locally was not nearly as dominant as it is today. The company had only about an 18 percent market share in St. Louis County. Falstaff, Stag, and Schlitz were dominant brands. It was not easy for a salesman to walk into a tavern and tell the owner, "I want you to take down your Falstaff sign and put up a Budweiser sign and start serving Budweiser on tap." It was a hard sell, because Falstaff had between 42 and 48 percent of the market.

Shortly after Tom and Mr. Busch agreed to split off St. Louis County and create an independent wholesaler, it was also decided to do the same thing with St. Louis City. Curt Lohr was the city sales branch manager at Anheuser-Busch and about ten months later, he was awarded the distributorship for the city.

A lot of space in the county was not developed in 1963, and there was a big difference between the markets of St. Louis County and St. Louis City. It was customary to establish markets by city and county, and this was an easy way to split the market. It wasn't long, however, before problems developed.

Curt was upset. He didn't think it was fair operating a market with less potential, and he complained to August Busch III. A meeting was set up with August, Tom, and Bob McNamara at the King Brothers Restaurant on Lindbergh and Highway 40. Mr. Busch said Anheuser-Busch would redraw the territories, probably more of an east-west split than city-county, and Tom got upset.

"You can't do that," Tom said. "I'm not going to let you do it. We have a signed agreement."

August was adamant. "We are going to change it and divide it another way," he said. I understood this to be the general tone of the meeting—that August didn't want one wholesaler with greater potential than the other.

Both Tom and August were angry, and the meeting broke up that way.

"Then I guess the next place I will see you is on the court-house steps," Tom said in finality.

That never happened, but there were bad feelings on both sides for years. Curt eventually died and left the operation to his two sons, Ron and Steve. Nobody ever brought up trying to re-divide the territories again as far as I know.

Protecting your territory always has been vitally important to a wholesaler's success, and it always was understood that one distributor never went into another distributor's territory to un-dersell him. That happened to me once.

I was in my office when I received a phone call from one of my drivers who said that somebody was trying to sell Anheuser-Busch beer to a liquor store in Lemay, Missouri, for fifty cents a case less than I could sell it. I immediately jumped in my car and sped to the store.

The driver for that distributor was still there, and when I asked where he was from, he wouldn't tell me. It was a rental truck with no wholesaler identification on the cab. I then asked the storeowner to show me the ticket for the beer he was buying from the driver, and he didn't want to do it.

"You can either show it to me, or you can show it to the liquor control officials," I told him. "This beer could have come from across the state line. Maybe the tax hasn't been paid on it."

He reluctantly showed me the ticket, and I saw it had come from Cape Girardeau, Missouri. I called the wholesaler when I got back to my office.

"Don't you ever do that again or you will look up and see one hundred Grey Eagle trucks coming into your territory, and I'll be selling beer for a dollar less than you can sell it for," I said.

Eventually, we were able to pass legislation in the state that protected a wholesaler's territory, and it really was in the best interests of the consumer. The local company is better able to service the retailer. That company can rotate the beer to make sure it is fresh. You can't monitor the product as well if you are not the frontline distributor.

In October 1963, Grey Eagle was able to move into a new building and put all of our operations under one roof, thanks to Ben Kerner, former owner of the St. Louis Hawks of the NBA. He put up the money to build the building and became our land-lord. That helped us get better organized. However, the biggest problem we faced was continuing labor relations. We did not have a mandatory arbitration clause in our contract, which had carried over from the Anheuser-Busch operation.

I worked in a variety of jobs on the production side and became the Warehouse and Delivery Manager. I knew we still were running a fairly inefficient operation and that we would have to do something about it to become a profitable business and properly support our brand trends. We went through some short strikes and actually lost money in three of our first eight years in business. We operated in the red basically because of our inability to handle the product efficiently, and that was be-cause of the strength of the union, which did not want to give up the soft and under-productive approach they had enjoyed at Anheuser-Busch.

We negotiated some minor load increases in the next few years, then a double load with a helper at the same pay. We saved the cost of a truck in the process.

In the old days, the brewery looked the other way if a driver stopped into a tavern and had a couple of beers on company time. They viewed this as promotion and as an attempt to talk the tavern owner into carrying more of the company's product. A big company could hide losses like that, but when you are a small company, you don't have any place to write off those kinds of expenses. The labor expense of overtime exceeded the value of the spending expense. A lack of productivity still kept our company from making a reasonable profit. We also still lacked a mandatory arbitration clause, which means if you have a serious disagreement, the union can strike the company at any time for any reason. Both of these issues had to be rectified in the future.

One morning Tom came into my office and asked if I would be interested in becoming the new sales manager.

The request surprised me, because I still didn't have any sales experience, and I was several years younger than most of the other salesmen in the company. Tom acknowledged that, but he also said he wanted me to take the job to have somebody in that position who could make good decisions and who had good communication skills.

"Do you think the other salesmen will accept me as the manager?" I asked Tom. He told me that he thought they would. That was important to me, because I didn't want to be in a position where I thought the people responsible to me would resent me. It needed to be a cooperative arrangement, and I needed to gain their confidence if we were going to be successful. I agreed to give it a try.

Tom was correct when he talked about the importance of having good communication skills. I admired people who had those skills. Look at some of the best politicians in our country over the last few decades. The most successful ones could communicate the best with the American people. Ronald Reagan was known as the "great communicator." He spoke in plain language that everyone could understand. People fail at communication when they use language as a tool to exhibit their education. Their subordinates can't fully understand the message being conveyed.

I had not been in the sales manager's job long when Tom told me we would have a management meeting the following day and that, as the new sales manager, I had to prepare a sales budget. I had to go through each brand for each month for the following year and project what our sales would be. I had to prepare a spreadsheet with all of our brands and packages for each month—no small task, but I accepted the challenge.

I went home and got out an old-style calculator, spread out all of my papers, and went to work. I worked all night on it, and I got it done. About 8 a.m. the following morning, I took a shower, shaved, and got dressed for work. When I made my presentation, the first thing the secretary-treasurer said to me was, "Who did this for you?"

I think it's natural for sales people to have some animosity for accountants, and vice versa. Bill Mraz and I were pretty good examples of this business relationship.

"I did it," I said. "I haven't been to bed since yesterday morning." I have to admit I really resented that question!

Doing the work gave me confidence, because I was able to achieve something and create something that did not exist before. I took the numbers, followed the historical patterns, and built a trend. It was mostly just logic, but the key was being able to present it and knowing exactly what I was talking about. We had a sales budget.

After that meeting I thought to myself, "This is a good example that you could accomplish most anything if you are willing to sacrifice the time and work hard."

Tom owned 70 percent of Grey Eagle, and his partner, Robert McNamara, owned 30 percent. I was just an employee with no ownership. I was still working twelve-plus hours a day, and I finally went to Tom and told him I would have to leave the company. I had moved up the ladder, taken on all assignments, and my contributions were critical to the success of the company.

I told him I was working too hard simply to earn a salary, and that I wanted a position where I could start building equity for my family. I told him I needed to go somewhere where I could have a share in the ownership of a company. I didn't want to work for simply two paychecks a month for the rest of my life.

Tom heard me out, and we went to lunch at the Bellerive Country Club to discuss the matter further. To keep me at Grey Eagle, he agreed to sell me 5 percent of his stock, with a promise that I could buy more at a later date. I liked what I was doing. This was the "deal" I needed, so I accepted it.

I had to go to the bank and borrow a little more than $100,000 to pay for the stock, and I spent the next five years paying off that loan. I didn't buy a new sports coat, shirt, or tie during that period. I always wore a white shirt, a tie, and jacket to work, because I believed dressing for the part was important. If I dressed professionally, I felt professional and acted in a professional manner. That was one of my personal codes of conduct, but it was hard to do when I was trying to pay off that loan. Some of my clothes became pretty threadbare. It was tough on Jo and the family with the amount of money going out of the house, but we got through it, and it was well worth it.

In the early 1970s the business was doing well, and our share of the market was climbing. I had been promoted again, to vice president, then general manager, and finally to executive vice president. I was in charge of almost all day-to-day operations of the company.

McNamara really was not that involved in the day-to-day business at that point. He had worked for the D'Arcy Advertising Agency in Chicago and had gotten to know Tom through his presentations and meetings with the brewery. He was primarily involved with market surveys and studies and worked a lot with outdoor billboard advertising. He became Grey Eagle's first director of sales and eventually moved into the more administrative side of the company.

Before I could get too comfortable with how well business was going, I found myself in the biggest professional fight of my still young career.

Chapter 4

THE MID-1970S BROUGHT EXTRA challenges for many businesses. Interest rates were high and fuel was scarce. There were long lines at gas stations across the nation. Health care costs and pensions, along with low productivity, were a hardship on companies in the brewing industry. Baby boomers were over twenty-one and taking positions in the job market, and demand grew for Anheuser-Busch products.

In early 1976, negotiations between Anheuser-Busch and the national Teamsters union broke down. Pickets went up at all Anheuser-Busch breweries. The strike was on.

The brewery needed to establish long-term goals concerning costs and productivity. The growth in the industry needed to be met with new brewing capacity, which required huge capital expenditures. It seemed the positions of the brewery and the union were polarized, and the strike dragged on.

The St. Louis beer wholesalers had formed an association for negotiation purposes, and I was asked to lead the group at the bargaining table. I accepted that challenge too, as we were the largest wholesaler, making our stake in the outcome higher.

Our local contract had expired at about the same time as the brewery's national contract. We kept negotiating with our local Teamsters, although health and welfare and pensions usually were determined by the brewery negotiations. Our focus was on productivity and wages. The big issue, however, was mandatory arbitration. The "right to strike" had taken its toll on the company over the years. We had an old-style labor business agent who loved to pound tables with his fist and chomp on cigars, and he usually made a strike threat about once a month.

All of the beer wholesalers had agreed that we could not run our businesses without being able to arbitrate our differences with the union.

One month into the national strike against Anheuser-Busch, Grey Eagle depleted its inventory of product. Our drivers now worked for my wholesale competition, filling the retail pipeline. As a result, the union played the waiting game with our negotiations. We were getting nowhere.

It was time to change tactics. We realized that as long as the drivers were working, we would never get a new contract. Knowing the "hot-headed" business agent would pull a quick trigger against us, I recommended that the "operating" wholesalers in our group load twenty extra cases onto each truck during their Sunday evening loading operation. Even though we had not asked a single driver to deliver the extra product, the business agent called a strike on each member of our association, including Grey Eagle, which had no product to sell. Now we had a level economic playing field for negotiation.

Federal mediator Michael O'Reilly was called in to oversee our negotiations. Three months had passed, and now we had a proposal hammered out to offer the union. It was mid-April, and we were about to enter the summer selling season.

With the brewery workers also still on strike, salaried employees and management personnel eventually shifted to production jobs so that Anheuser-Busch could begin producing beer again. I didn't buy any of the beer they produced, because I didn't have any drivers to deliver it. The drivers also were on strike, and more important, we had a new proposal on the table.

We had some incidents of violence, including Tom Burrows' house being firebombed. Luckily nobody was home when it happened. His daughter had just left the house, or she could easily have been asleep and killed. Their pet dog was killed. I was worried the longer the strike went on, the more violence there could be, and we were doing our best to try to negotiate a settlement with a new contract. It was never determined who was responsible for the firebombing, but we thought we could have made an educated guess.

Two Anheuser-Busch employees, Ron Rizzo and Jay Rideout, walked into my office one day and sat down. They told me I was in violation of the wholesaler equity agreement. Rizzo was the division manager from St. Louis, and Rideout was the regional manager from Houston.

"Would you explain that to me?" I said.

They said I was not doing my utmost to sell their product.

"I don't know if you noticed or not when you entered the building, but you crossed picket lines—my company is on strike," I said.

They said, "Yes, but we have beer to sell, and you have decided not to order any of the beer and sell it."

"Let me see if I've got this straight," I said. "You come in my office and notify me that I am in violation of my equity agreement when you know my partner's house was firebombed. You know I've been negotiating this contract for weeks and weeks. You don't ask about my people and their families or the principals of this company or their families. You don't ask if I'm close to a settlement of the contract. Your mission here is to put the hammer on me to sell beer. I'm the largest wholesaler in the community—they (the union) have to stop me if they are going to win this war. Is that your message today?"

They said yes.

"OK, get out of here, get out of my office, and get off the premises," I said.

I was really mad. They forced me to take a trailer load of beer from the brewery. Because Lohr operated only in the city, they had a shorter distance to travel and could secure better police protection for their trucks. We had to go through several municipalities in the county, and even though we thought we had secured good protection for our trucks and hired a nonunion driver, I feared something might happen.

The union did its best to stop the truck from getting through.

It was reported they tried to drop boulders off the viaducts on the highway as the truck drove under them. As the truck headed for our office, the number of picketers outside the office increased to about 150 to 200 people. Many were standing at the end of the street, in the cul de sac, drinking beer all morning.

Tom Burrows had called and wanted me to come to a meeting away from the office, but before I left I talked to the St. Louis County police officer who was in charge, Captain Graves, and asked why he was allowing the people to drink beer at the end of the street where my trucks had to pass. "They seem to be getting intoxicated, and it's going to be a problem," I said.

He said he would look into it, and I left to go meet with Tom.

When I was at the meeting, the trailer showed up, and as I expected, there was trouble. One guy swung a baseball bat, and another tried to throw some kind of liquid into the cab. The driver tried to swerve to get out of the way, and he lost control of the truck. He cut the wheel sharply to the right, and the truck flipped over. Twenty-two hundred cases of Budweiser went flying through the roof.

My secretary called and said there was a near riot going on outside the office. The striking drivers had jumped on top of the overturned truck and were dancing and swinging baseball bats and clubs. Luckily the driver had scrambled out of the truck and made it into the office, where he was safe. My secretary said the striking drivers were calling my name, wanting me to come out and talk to them.

"Let me talk to Graves," I said. She got him on the phone.

"It sounds to me like you've got this thing totally out of hand now," I said.

He said, "Well, I'd advise you not to come back here right now."

"Oh, I'm coming back," I said. "I have people in that building, and I'm concerned about your ability to keep them safe. If there is something I can do to help provide for their safety I'm going to do it." He said he was going to put a police car at the end of the street, off Page Avenue, to escort me to the office.

"You can do whatever you want, but I will be there in less than ten minutes," I said and hung up the phone.

I had a pistol in the glove compartment of my car, and as I got close to the street I reached into the glove compartment and pulled it out. As I turned onto the street, I couldn't believe the scene. It was a foggy and rainy day, with a really eerie sky, and it looked as if World War III had broken out in front of the office.

The police officer stopped my car and told me he was going to follow me down the street to the office.

"You're going to follow me down?" I said. "Well, you better stay far enough back that you don't get hurt."

He saw the pistol sitting on the front seat and said, "Now don't you be using that pistol unless you really need to."

I told him, "I will take care of my business; you take care of yours."

I thought for sure I was going to get shot as I drove down the street to the office. I was going about five miles an hour, and I held the pistol up so the people could see it. I was prepared for a flash, which would be the first sign somebody had shot at me. I was going to bail out of the car and start shooting, because I was determined not to go down without a fight.

The striking drivers had blocked the entrance to the company's parking lot, but as I eased the car toward it, the drivers backed off and there was no violence. I parked and went into the office, where Graves was waiting.

"What is your plan?" I asked.

He said he was going to call in the SWAT team and line the street so our people could get out and go home. I told him it wasn't much of a gesture and it was a little too late but it was what we would have to do.

I called everyone into the conference room and said, "We're going to suspend operations of the company because of the situation. You all go home, and you will remain on the payroll for as long as I can keep you on the payroll. If you have any harassment in any way to you or your family or your home, you call me and let me know. I will provide protection."

Everyone got out of the office and made it home safely. I was the last to leave and made it home without any trouble. Jo was standing in the kitchen, and her back was to me as I came into the house.

"Jo, everything erupted today," I said. She said, "I know, I saw it all on television. It was awful." Channel 2, the ABC affiliate at the time, had remained behind and had filmed everything. As she turned around, tears were running down her face.

I said, "I'm going to ask you to take the boys, Jeff and Brian, and go up to your mother's house in Wisconsin until this settles down. I don't know what is going to happen. I need you to go away where I know you and the boys will be safe. I think everything is only going to get tougher."

She said she already had called the airline, and they had reservations on a flight that evening. Tom Burrows came over, and together we drove my wife and kids to the airport. It was very tough to kiss my two little boys goodbye when they should have been in bed in the comfort and safety of their home.

Jo said to Tom, "Take care of him." Tom said, "Jo, he's taking care of all of us."

I went home, and even though it was after midnight, there was no way I was going to sleep. I picked up the telephone and started calling some of my striking drivers, knowing I was going to be waking them up.

"Jim, you want to talk to me? This is Jerry Clinton," I said. "I heard you yell something at me today when I drove into the office. If you've got something to say to me, get up right now and meet me at the east end of the bridge to St. Charles on I-70. I will meet you on the east side of the bridge and we'll have our little talk. You also had better bring a weapon with you, because I have a weapon."

He said, "I don't want to talk to you."

"Then let me tell you something," I said. "When I drive into my office you had better be looking the other way, because I don't want to see you. I don't want you to say anything to me because you have a bunch of guys there with you egging you on. If you and I are going to talk, we are going to do it one on one."

I repeated basically this same message to four or five other drivers and got the same response each time. It made the entrance and exit to my company a lot easier in the days to come.

We did have some sporadic violence. I thought somebody shot at me one time as I was driving down the street. I heard what I thought was a pistol shot but didn't see anything. Another time I was almost run off the highway into a bridge abutment. A car came at me from the rear at high speed, and I know it was intentional. I didn't get the license plate number. Needless to say, our proposal was voted down.

We finally had to put nonunion drivers in the trucks, and that brought the negotiations with the union back to day one. I really thought before Rizzo and Rideout came to my office we had a decent chance of getting a contract negotiated, but when that happened, all bets were off. The brewery had made the wrong move by forcing my hand.

The strike went on for four months, and I really think one of the reasons we managed to settle it was because of a conversation at the National Teamsters Convention in Las Vegas. The national president had a meeting with our business agent and asked how the problem in St. Louis was coming along. The agent reportedly told the president that the negotiations were progressing, but the president said, "That's not what I hear. I hear the kid is kicking your ass."

I was the kid, since I was all of thirty-nine years old at the time.

The president wanted to know what the main issue was, which was our insistence on the inclusion of a mandatory arbitration clause in the contract.

I was told the president of the national Teamsters union said, "We have mandatory arbitration all over the country. Why do you think you're so special in St. Louis? You'd better get back there and settle the issue."

I was at home on a Sunday afternoon when my lawyer, Allen Berger, called and said, "The boys are back from Las Vegas, and they want to meet and talk."

"That's good," I said, "I'll look at my schedule tomorrow when I get in the office, and we'll set something up in the next couple of weeks."

"They want to meet today," my lawyer said.

I tried to explain that it was Sunday, that I was at home with my family, and that I didn't want to come to a meeting. He insisted and said that he thought they were under orders from the national union to settle the strike. I finally agreed to come down.

The union guys were Chubby Taylor and John Girard. The minute I walked into the meeting room, they started pounding the table and cussing. I told them exactly what I thought of them and that they could take the contract and stick it where the sun doesn't shine, that I was doing just fine delivering my beer with nonunion drivers.

I then got up and walked out of the room. My lawyer came out after me and begged me to come back in and talk to them. I didn't think it would do any good, but I went back into the room. Before I left again, we had mandatory arbitration and five other issues agreed to, and the union went back to work.

One of the difficult results of the strike was that eleven drivers went to jail or were fined for violating court-issued restraining orders. I sat in the courtroom for the judgments. One side of the room was filled with the drivers and their friends. I was on the other side of the room. Some of the drivers were fined as much as $8,000 to $10,000 and were sent directly off to jail. Others were fined $1,000 to $2,000, and the jail sentences ran as long as forty-five days. I felt bad for the drivers and their families, but there was hard evidence that they had attacked our trucks and had forced them off the road. They had thrown tacks on driveways, shot out windows of stores with ball bearings, and dumped concrete in the urinals of our retail businesses. Those actions could not be ignored.

From that point in time to today, we have enjoyed labor peace, a period of more than thirty years.

It was the turning point of my life. I became the president of Grey Eagle, and that opened up additional opportunities for the company. I could implement a lot of changes in our operation that I had been thinking about over the years. I knew these changes would benefit our business and our employees.

Burrows' health had deteriorated, and he wanted to retire and get out of the company. McNamara and I agreed to buy him out and become equal partners. As great a guy as Tom was, and as much of a mentor as he was to me, he had never developed the relationship that he wanted with the drivers. Tom wanted to be one of the boys, and he tried to hold meetings on Saturdays and showed up in jeans and a denim shirt to show them that he was just "one of the guys."

I tried to tell him, "Tom they don't want to be your friend. They want to be your employee. They know you are not going to invite them over to your house for dinner Saturday night, and they would be uncomfortable there to begin with. They want you to be their boss. You have to act like it."

He didn't always buy that. He had dinner dances and bought gifts for the driver's wives, but nothing he tried improved his relationship with the drivers, so he wanted out. Tom had been my mentor and was a good teacher. We spent many hours together with Bob McNamara deep-sea fishing and talking about business. He died in 1994 while undergoing a heart operation in Florida.

When Tom wanted to leave Grey Eagle, McNamara and I agreed to give him all of the cash we had in the business and all of the money we could borrow. We were left with about $25,000 cash in the company. We also agreed that I would buy

McNamara's half of the company in ten years and pay the debt off over the next ten years. He would be retirement age by then, and this would ensure his position and earnings for twenty years, or past his normal retirement age.

Given the autonomy to make the changes I wanted to make, we set up an automatic computer routing system for our trucks, started tracking the payables and receivables by computer, and went to a pre-sell system, hiring people to call our customers and sell the beer before the cases were placed on the truck. That way, when the trucks left the loading dock in the morning, every case of beer on the truck had been pre-sold. We didn't have drivers going out in the morning trying to peddle their beer, not knowing how many cases they would sell or how many they would bring back to the office at the end of the day.

We also bought all of our trucks instead of leasing them. My old friend Don Sorich had left the company and was running a motorcycle shop near Crystal City, but I talked him into coming back as our fleet manager. It was not a tough sell. We negotiated higher load limits with delivery commissions for the drivers, and that increased our productivity and utilized our equipment better. It also provided greater earnings for our drivers.

I also increased the community awareness of our company by sponsoring sports and athletic events around town and by becoming involved in many charitable activities. We became a sponsor of the Golden Gloves, and we started the Budweiser Sports Apartment League, which eventually grew to about 15,000 participants playing a wide variety of sports on teams from their apartment complexes. The idea was that after the games, they would go to their local bar or tavern and consume our product, building brand loyalty. That was exactly what happened. The program spread to other cities because it was so successful.

With the help of Michael Drolich, a public relations executive, we were the first company in the industry to introduce an anti-drinking-and-driving program, called "None for the

Road." We distributed materials through the high school driver's education classes and the local police departments. I was very proud of that program. Colonel Gil Kleinknecht, chief of the St. Louis County police, was on my advisory board and helped by placing our special logo-designed bumper stickers on all police vehicles.

Many people have the opinion that owning a beer distributorship, much less an Anheuser-Busch distributorship, is like having a license to steal. The fact is, it depends where you are operating this business. In St. Louis, it's tough for many reasons. For one, it is the home brewery market for local A-B distributors. This means there could be 6,000-plus direct employees living in the market, in addition to the Busch family and top executives of the brewery. They all shop and interact with our "customers"— supermarkets, drug stores, restaurants, taverns, etc. If they don't find the package of one of our brands or the date of packaging (born-on dating) does not appeal to their delicate palates, they may register a complaint.

These complaints are usually handled by the local A-B field-sales office in our district. This necessitates our sales people being called from their daily routes to investigate what usually turns out to be a bogus complaint. Any lack of product at the retail level generally resulted from a lack of ability to pay for previously bought products, or from the store's inability to keep their shelves stocked from the supply in their own back storeroom. All of this was counterproductive for the wholesaler. Product rotation was of utmost importance to the wholesaler, since we all signed agreements to strictly enforce the shelf life established by our supplier, Anheuser-Busch. Should the product exceed their maximum shelf-life period, it must be picked up by the wholesaler with credit to the retailer. This product is then destroyed at the wholesaler's expense. The expense is not only the cost of the product, but it also must include the cost of warehousing, loading, delivering, and picking up the product. The process is expensive in a Teamsters market.

A few years ago, Anheuser-Busch established a "Bud Hotline" where any consumer anywhere could call a toll-free phone number and get answers to questions or file complaints about any of our products. The company soon learned to separate the bogus calls from the legitimate calls, which produced a better form of consumer communication.

There is another reason beer wholesaling is a tougher business than many people think—it's not a "right to own" business. It is a privilege granted by local, state, and the federal governments as stipulated by the 21st Amendment to the U.S. Constitution. This privilege can be revoked at any time for due cause. Your license can be suspended for a period of time as determined by the supervisor of liquor control on the local level, or the Bureau of Alcohol, Tobacco and Firearms on the federal level. Should an employee commit an infraction without your knowledge, the millions of dollars you have invested in your business could be seriously jeopardized.

The infraction could result from a driver selling an order of beer to a retailer with a revoked license (where the driver failed to physically check the license at the point of the sale). Or the driver might have sold product to a customer who was delinquent in paying his last bill. With hundreds of sales a day and hundreds of thousands a year, it still is the wholesaler's responsibility to monitor each sale.

Another problem is the political concerns that could seriously affect your business. I believe the pressures on the alcohol beverage industry are well known. Special-interest groups across the country are working day and night to outlaw the sale of our products again. Their lobbyists are working on legislation and the public at every level to obtain their goals.

History shows that Prohibition was a total disaster, causing lost revenue and jobs at every level. Meanwhile, untaxed alcohol was being sold at record levels illegally, without tax or controls. Therefore, industry members must be able to communicate with lawmakers on both sides of the aisle to maintain their right to do business. This process is time-consuming and expensive but absolutely necessary. Otherwise, small pieces of legislation could produce increases in taxes of the product, restrictions to retail license holders, reductions in the number of days to sell and service the product, and who knows what else?

As strange as it may seem, open and free competition is close to the bottom of a wholesaler's business plan, insofar as daily pressures are concerned. The right to wholesale beer is hardly a license to steal.

Still, we were lucky and our business was growing and doing well, making us more confident in ourselves. Any time you have success, it gives you a feeling that you can achieve even more. With the company going strong, I began to look for new challenges.

After I had settled in as the sole owner of Grey Eagle in the early 1980s, I made another acquisition that I thought would be beneficial to the employees of my company. I found a beautiful two hundred-acre property in Warren County just forty-five miles west of the Grey Eagle office.

This property offered five bedrooms, a great room, and a finished walkout basement. A horse barn and four bodies of water were included. The largest was a fish-stocked eighteen-acre spring-fed lake located only slightly more than one hundred yards down a slopping hill from the residence. It was a beautiful recreational property with even greater potential.

Having grown up in the inner city, I thought it would be great for my employees to be able to bring their children to "Eagle Estate" and enjoy catching their first fish with their parents, or take their first horseback ride, or just swim in the pool that I planned to provide at a later date.

Over the next two decades, I enhanced the property with many additions for the comfort and pleasure of my guests. The house was located approximately one-half mile from the front gate, which is electronically controlled, meaning that once you enter the property you literally can lock the world out. It was a perfect retreat.

In 1983, I began a tradition that many will remember . . . the Grey Eagle picnic. The guest list included salaried employees and families, Anheuser-Busch executives, employees of companies that provided services to Grey Eagle, politicians, and selected friends. Mayor Vince Schoemehl and County Executive Buzz Westfall and families were regular guests. The total crowd always numbered nearly four hundred people.

I usually had a theme for the picnic, such as the "Hawaiian Luau" or the "Mexican Fiesta" or even "A Fair to Remember," my last party in 2005, which featured a fifty-foot Ferris Wheel. The kids loved it, including those kids fifty years of age or older.

My most extravagant party was the celebration of Grey Eagle's 25th anniversary in 1987.

This one was a sit-down dinner under a huge tent. After dinner the guests were directed to theater-style seating down the sloping hill toward the lake, under the stars. I had a stage moved from the Missouri State Fair in Sedalia and reconstructed at Eagle Estate. I went to the stage and announced that the entertainment for the evening was Doc Severson and the NBC Orchestra from The Tonight Show. I was honored to have August III fly in on his helicopter with his wife Jenny and their two children to celebrate with us. It was a great night in a perfect setting.

Back in 1982 I had a beer truck driver named Larry Schob, who was an avid horseman. Since I wanted to offer horseback riding, I needed to hire someone to manage the property who knew how to care for the horses. Larry brought out a young woman acquaintance, Rosie Ring, as an applicant. Rosie was hired and still has the same job more than two decades later. She was just twenty-two at the time.

The team I put together to produce these events were Rosie, Jim Hubbard (my administrative assistant), and Mike Drohlich, my PR director. They always did a great job of presenting the event I had designed.

We also used the format to present service awards to our employees who were observing their 5th, 10th, 15th, 20th, 25th, and even 30th year of employment. My son Jeff used to enjoy bringing each recipient up to the podium and making a personal remark complimenting their service. Jeff was much loved by the employees, and it showed. The only time since 1983 we did not hold this event was, understandably, in 2002, when Jeff lost his life. For the second-to-last event, thanks to Steve Shankman of Contemporary Productions, we featured Michael Buble and his orchestra. I also invited my old pal, Ed McMahon.

In all those years of producing an outdoor event, we were never rained out.

My old friends Keith Wortman, a former Cardinal football lineman, and Kay White were married at the lake's edge in 1986. It was a beautiful and fun event. I had Rosie drive the bride from the house to the lake in my carriage, pulled by my white Arabian horse.

Keith's former coach and my pal, Jim Hanifan, was there along with many of Keith's former teammates, including Dan Dierdorf. The reception eventually moved to the pool and patio area, and even though we were enjoying another great event with no rain, it did get a little wet.

As boys will be boys, the pool offered too much temptation. The first to get pushed in was Dan, tux and all. Then it was fair game, with myself, Keith, Hanifan, and others taking an unscheduled dip. When Dan went in the second time, the situation got a little tense. Fortunately someone suggested it was time to cut the cake. Thank goodness, Eagle Estate remained intact.

From time to time I run into a person in their twenties who tells me what great memories he has as a young child coming to the Grey Eagle picnics with his parents. Those memories last forever. For me it was a great opportunity to share our success with the people who helped achieve it.

Chapter 5

GREY EAGLE HAD BECOME INVOLVED with automobile racing, on a small scale, as another way to promote the company and the Budweiser brand. We sponsored a couple of
cars involved in local racing and became more involved
when one of the drivers, Dr. Terry McKenna, a dentist,
began to have some success. He went on to win three national championships driving a Grey Eagle Budweiser car.

I had never been interested in auto racing before, and my
interest now was limited to how the advertising exposure would
help increase sales. I went out to the track one time because our
second car was having trouble finishing races, and I thought, "I
could at least finish." We were not getting enough advertising
exposure for our expense if the car was not making enough laps
around the track, much less winning races.

It was about this time I met Paul Newman, the actor turned
racecar driver, and my interest in racing grew tremendously.

Newman was coming to the St. Louis area to compete in a
Sports Car Club of America event at the Mid-America Raceway
in Wentzville. Budweiser sponsored Newman's car, and I received a call from the advertising agency asking if I could bring
my motor home out to the racetrack for Newman to use during
the weekend. They wanted to keep him out of the hot weather
and away from some of the crowds.

I decided it was a good opportunity to meet Newman, so I
went out for the race and we struck up a conversation. He asked
how old I was, and I told him I was forty-five. He told me he was
forty-six the first time he drove a racecar. He said, "You still have
time to do it."

I still was not convinced—until I actually got behind the wheel of a Datsun B210 racecar for a few laps at the Mid-America track in 1982. We were considering buying the car, and I wanted to see how it ran, or rather how I handled it. Jeff was nineteen at the time and went with me and watched as I made a few laps.

The view I had most of the time during my practice laps was out the side window of the car; I kept getting the car sideways in almost every corner. When I finished the practice runs, I got out of the car and said, "OK, we'll buy the car." It was a rather old car and didn't cost much money.

I tossed Jeff the keys to my Ferrari and asked him to drive us home. "I've got a lot on my mind," I said. During the trip, we sat in silence for several moments until Jeff finally spoke up.

"What are you doing?" he said.

"What do you mean, what am I doing?" I answered.

"Buying that racecar, thinking you can drive it," he said. "You're going to hurt yourself."

"I'm going to win some races," I said.

Jeff wasn't convinced. "Knowing you, you probably will win some races," he said. He still was very much against me getting involved in racing as a driver.

If I was going to get involved in racing, I was determined to go about it the right way. I enrolled at the Bob Bondurant School of High Performance Driving at Sears Point, California, where they put you through four intense days of driving instruction. It may look easy watching a race at home on television or even in person at a track, but there really is a high degree of skill involved in driving a racecar, and it isn't something you can do without taking the proper training.

Most of the instruction had to do with understanding the balance and the weight transfers of a car, as well as the braking points and how to deal with turns. You have to work up to the speeds involved and train your mind as well as your body, because the reaction time is the most critical skill involved in racing. If you just jump in a car and want to drive 150 miles an hour, it is hard for your mind to react at that rate. You might be able to do it in a straight line, but you have to know when to brake and slow down to handle the turns by identifying the apex of the corner. That's something the guy on the street doesn't always understand.

One week after completing the training, I entered a Sports Car Club of America race at the Hallett Motor Speedway in Oklahoma and was lucky enough to win the race. I was then officially hooked. Our only problem was we couldn't go out and drink a Bud to celebrate because the racetrack was in a dry county.

My second race was going to be near St. Louis at the Mid-America track in Wentzville, and I was really determined not to make it a big deal. I didn't want any publicity; I wanted just to sneak into the sport. Mostly I was afraid I would embarrass myself in front of a bunch of retail customers and employees. I could picture them saying, "Look at that idiot out there."

A few days before the race, I received a phone call from a reporter from *Fortune* magazine. Marilyn Wellemeyer was a writer for a section of the magazine known as "On Your Own Time." She told me she wanted to come in and write about my race.

"Paul Newman is going to be here," I said. "Why don't you write about him?"

She said no, they wanted to write about why a businessman was getting involved in racing. It seems to be a trend, she said. "We want to write about you," she said.

So much for sneaking into the sport. The story came out with the headline, "Vroom at the Top."

I was lucky enough to be named Rookie of the Year for the St. Louis region in 1983, an honor that later both my sons, Jeff and Brian, also would achieve. I won six times in 1984, and won six of ten races in 1985.

I admitted in a newspaper interview the most enjoyable part of racing was winning.

"Sometimes, it's almost like a disease," I said. "I can't stand to be in second place in anything."

Most of my races were on the regional scale, with the small cars, before I eventually moved into a higher class of cars. The Pro Trans Am Racing Series was where I found myself competing against Newman and some other famous racers. There, I learned humility in racing.

We entered a 500-horsepower Ford Mustang in the Twelve Hours of Sebring endurance race, where people like A.J. Foyt, Bobby Rahal, and Danny Ongais were competing. Usually, three drivers were on a team. There are three or four classes of cars in the race, so there are class winners as well as the overall champion. Our team finished 13th overall out of seventy-four cars in the race. It was like being a minor-league baseball player and getting to play on the same team with Stan Musial. In twelve hours, our car covered 1,052 miles.

Our team consisted of Morris Clement, a local driver from Belleville, Illinois, Stan Barrett, and myself. I took the third shift in the car, which was at night. I got into the car while we were changing all four tires during a pit stop and really was not ready for what would happen.

Our crew forgot to tape up the back window, so when I got on the track, I was having trouble seeing because of all of the headlights of the cars behind me. Then our radio stopped working, so I could not communicate with the crew. About halfway through my shift, I started hearing a grinding sound on my right front wheel. It sounded like a wheel bearing was going out, and it kept getting worse.

Because the radio was out, I could not talk to my crew to let them know what was going on. I just kept going, but finally the noise got so bad I decided I would go one more lap and then bring the car into the pits. I had no idea what lap I was on. When I pulled into the pits, the crew hooked up the pneumatic air hose and jacked the car up. As the car was being raised, the right front wheel literally fell off the car.

I would never have been able to make it through one more turn. The car most likely would have skidded into the corner and I would have had a horrific crash. What had happened was that when Stan had been racing in the afternoon, he had hit a curb and gone off the track. I didn't know that. The impact had left a crack all the way around the wheel, and it went unnoticed when Goodyear mounted a new tire to be used later in the race. I was lucky enough to get that wheel for my shift! It just gradually broke off. I learned that was what had happened from a picture in the newspaper the following day. Stan Barrett would never admit a slow-speed mistake after breaking the speed of sound in a Budweiser rocket car at 739.666 miles an hour during a run at Edwards Air Force Base on December 17, 1979.

Our team had a very respectable finish, fourth in our class, but I was more grateful we had made it safely through the race.

At another race, the Grand Prix through the streets of Detroit, I was running seventh with only eight laps to go when I was forced to drop out because of engine trouble. During a practice preceding the race, Paul Newman stopped by my motor coach with a bunch of bananas in his hand.

My son Brian excitedly said, "Dad, Paul Newman is here with a bunch of bananas."

"It's OK, Brian," I said, "You can let Butch Cassidy in."

Newman held out the bananas and said, "I want you to have enough potassium for the race, and I have something I want to talk to you about," Newman said. I knew immediately the subject wasn't racing.

I certainly was interested and willing to listen.

Newman explained how he was trying to raise money to finance a camp he wanted to build in Connecticut for children hospitalized with catastrophic illnesses, to give them a place where they could retreat and be kids again for a while. He called it the "Hole in the Wall Gang" camp. The children were going to have horseback rides, wagon rides, canoes, campfire sing-alongs—activities that could take their minds off the hospital for a couple of weeks. Yale University would provide for their on-site medical needs.

I could see Paul's eyes glistening as he talked, and it was obvious he was on a personal mission. "What can I do to help?" I asked.

He explained that all money earned by his food company went to charity, but his accountants had told him he needed matching funds to accomplish his goals for the camp. He was trying to solicit corporate support to get the camp buildings built and wanted to know if I could arrange a meeting for him with August Busch III. It so happened we were having a wholesaler's meeting the next week, and I told Newman I would see what I could do.

A few days later, I told August I needed to see him after the meeting, and he invited me to his office. Paul had given me some printed materials about the camp and also a video he had put together. August told me to put on the tape, and obviously Paul did a good sales job on the film, since he has had more than a little acting experience.

After the video was over, August looked at me and said, "He's a good guy, isn't he?" and I responded, "Yes he is, and I will tell you something else, he's a Budweiser drinker."

August told me to arrange for Paul to come in to St. Louis and "bring his laundry list" of what he wanted. August would meet with him to discuss the project. We set up the meeting, and I met Paul at Parks Airport in Illinois.

It turned out he had lost a filling in a tooth on the flight to St. Louis, so we had to stop at a dentist's office in an East St. Louis "strip center" so he could get it fixed before the meeting. When we walked into the office and the receptionist and nurse saw who it was, they ran down to the corner drugstore and bought a throwaway camera so they could take a picture of Paul in the dentist's chair.

The meeting was with August, Mike Roarty, Jerry Ritter, Paul, and myself. Paul explained his needs for the corporate funding and how he was trying to get various corporations to underwrite half the cost for each building.

"What is your largest building," August asked.

Paul said it was the "round house" dining room facility, projected to cost about $1.3 million. He explained that his food company would pick up half of that cost. August looked at him and said, "We'll give you the other half, $650,000, to build the facility."

Paul looked across the table at me and said, "Is this it?" and I said, "No, Paul, this is where you say, 'Thank you Mr. Busch.'"

"Oh gosh, yes," Paul said. "I really do thank you. I just didn't think corporations could give money like that without a lot of meetings."

I said, "Not this corporation. When Mr. Busch says he will give you $650,000 for this charitable event, you've got $650,000."

Newman was appreciative, and August added, "There is one catch. You have to invite Jerry and me up to the camp when you have the grand opening." He agreed to do that.

As we were leaving Busch's office, I could see the rings of sweat under Paul's armpits. I could not believe how heavily he was perspiring, and I said something to him about it. "You look worse than when you come out of a racecar," I said.

"I've never asked corporations like this for money before," Newman said. "It's the first time I've ever done something like this, and I was scared to death."

We stopped at a store on the way back to the airport and bought a case of Budweiser for the celebration dinner with his wife Joanne upon his return home.

August and I went to the grand opening, and it was just a marvelous facility. I had been out a little late the night before our departure, but I figured August would fly the corporate jet himself, and I could get a couple hours of rest, but no, he sat across from me with a large file of marketing surveys and for two hours asked my opinion of each one. However, he did fly us home. My much-needed rest came late that day.

Newman has since built even more camps in other locations, and they are a wonderful resource for hundreds of children.

One of the most enjoyable aspects of being involved in racing was meeting and becoming friends with people like

Newman. He was an outstanding racecar driver, and I enjoyed his friendship.

We were both racing one weekend in a Pro Trans Am race at Road America in Elkhart Lake, Wisconsin. The state of Wisconsin is loaded with small supper clubs on every road and highway in the state. One of the best is Miller's Supper Club, which sits just outside the gate to Road America. They serve a walleyed pike, a huge filet of fish battered and deep fried. When you break open the batter, the white tender fish is absolutely delicious. I looked forward to eating there every time we were at Road America, and we made reservations for our crew to dine there after the practice sessions on Friday.

After a practice run, I was relaxing in my motor home, getting ready to shower and to dress for dinner, when there was a knock on the door. It was Newman's crew chief, inviting us to have dinner at his trailer. He was barbequing his "world-famous hamburgers." He insisted the meat be something like 28 percent fat so it would make a perfect burger.

"I'm sorry, tell Paul I appreciate the offer very much but we have already made reservations at Miller's Supper Club," I said. "I will take a rain-check if he will give it to me."

The crew chief left but was back within a few minutes.

"Paul understands," he said. "He said he has been turned down before. He at least wants you to come over and have some hors d'oeuvres before you go to dinner."

"Great," I said. "We would love to do that."

I finished getting showered and dressed, then our crew went over to Newman's trailer. He had our "hors d'oeuvres" waiting— paper plates full of chunks of hamburger cut into little pieces with a toothpick sticking out of them. That was our hors d'oeuvres.

Being an Anheuser-Busch distributor helped open many doors for me, both in the business world and in racing. One project that combined both activities was when I became involved in the attempt by Hal Needham and Stan Barrett to break the land-speed record driving the Budweiser rocket car in 1979.

Needham was a successful movie director and, coincidentally, had also gone to Hadley Tech High School, although a few years earlier than me. Barrett was another former St. Louisan and one of the leading stunt men in Hollywood. Stan's mother had owned Barrett's Flower Shop at 141 and Olive for many years. Stan had worked in many of Hal's movies, doing a lot of the stunt double work for Burt Reynolds, who had been Hal's roommate in Hollywood for ten years during their single days.

Hal was looking for major sponsorships for their attempt to break the land-speed record as well as the sound barrier, and I helped him work out a deal with Anheuser-Busch. Hal actually was the only private citizen in the United States to own several Sidewinder missiles, because he had bought them from the government to use in his experiment.

Several of the early test runs were at the Bonneville Salt Flats in Utah, but eventually the rocket car got too fast and caused the salt to break up. Everyone was afraid the car would "tricycle" and crash. Needham was also friends with Chuck Yeager, the retired Air Force general who was the first to break the sound barrier in the Bell X.1 jet, and he used that connection to move the rocket-car tests to the Rogers dried lakebeds at Edwards Air Force Base in California.

It looked as if they would have a real chance of breaking the record, but the problem now was that Hal was down to his last two sidewinder missiles. The way the car was designed, a hybrid rocket ignited the car, and when it reached a rate of speed just under the speed of sound, Stan ignited the sidewinder missile, which propelled the car through the barrier. It takes twice the speed to go through the barrier as it does to reach it. Stan was attempting to break the speed of sound in a wheeled vehicle for the first time in history.

We knew they were down to their last couple of attempts. If they failed, everything would have to be put on hold for at least a year, and if they did not obtain additional financing, cancellation was possible.

One of Stan's problems was that when the car approached that level of speed—several hundred miles an hour—he couldn't see where he was going. Dave Mungenast, a car dealer in St. Louis and a friend of mine, had gone with me to California to watch the last record-breaking attempts. We both saw that Stan needed a visual point that he could focus on, so Dave and I went out early one morning and painted a line for two-and-a-half miles straight down the lake so Stan could have a better chance of keeping the car in a straight line.

Early on the morning of December 17, Stan was ready for his last attempt. It was cool, and everyone was nervous. He got on the public address system at first morning light and said a prayer. He got in the car, and nobody knew what was going to happen.

The hybrid rocket ignited and the car blasted off. When it reached speed, the sidewinder missile fired on cue. It was a sight like you would never see in your life. A huge ball of fire ignited and the car literally went out of sight from our vantage.

All of us piled in cars and raced down the track after Stan, and we realized that Stan had somehow kept the car under control. It took a while for the Air Force to calculate, through triangulation, the speed using radar, but later that day they determined Stan and the car had reached a speed of 739.666 miles an hour, breaking the land-speed record as well as the sound barrier. It was an unbelievable accomplishment, especially when we walked his path and realized the two rear wheels lifted when he hit the barrier. Miracle of miracles, they sat down approximately 300 feet down the track at exactly the same moment. Therefore, he went through the barrier on the nose-wheel.

One disappointment was that the National Hot Rod Association would not sanction the speed of the car under their specific rules, which would have required the car to turn around, refuel, race back down the track, and reach a calculated speed as an average of the two runs. Lack of fuel made this impossible.

There still was a great deal of recognition and publicity for Stan and everybody involved. He was featured on two

CBS television specials. The Budweiser rocket car went on a world tour and ended up in the Smithsonian Institution in Washington, D.C. I was glad to have been involved and even more thankful that I had been there to witness it in person.

Another person I met through racing, and became good friends with, was former NFL star Walter Payton.

I think Walter got into racing for many of the same reasons I got involved. He obviously was a fierce competitor, and after his NFL career ended, he was looking for other challenges and excitement. A friend got him hooked on racing. We ended up becoming teammates racing identical Ford Mustang Cobras owned by former Indy car driver Tom Gloy. Of course, Budweiser and the NFL sponsored us.

I had a little edge on Walter in experience, but he didn't like anybody having an edge on him. One time we were at the Sears Point track testing our new Mustang Cobras. We were walking out of the hotel that morning, and I asked him if he had ever driven that track before. He said no.

"Well, you have to understand this is a difficult track," I told him. "You have to take it slow for several laps and learn the track. Memorize the turns and all the nuances. There are a myriad of things you have to look out for. Take four, five, or six laps at a slower speed so you can get the feel of the track."

We suited up and headed for our cars. I was on my second lap when my crew chief came on the radio and told me there was a red flag, which meant to stop racing because of a wreck. I looked in my rear view mirror, and I couldn't see Walter. We had been the only two cars on the track. "Where's Walter?" I said on the radio.

"He went off the track in turn six," my crew chief said.

I coasted around the track until I saw what had happened. He had gone into turn six going too fast, and had overcorrected so he wouldn't leave the right side of the track. Instead, he went off the left side of the track, hit the ditch, and flipped the car over. I pulled up, jumped out of my car, and ran toward him.

Walter was lying on his back with his eyes closed. Water in the ditch was flowing beneath him. I grabbed him by the collar of his racing suit.

"Walter can you hear me, can you hear me?" I yelled. I knew he had to have crawled through the window of his car to get where he was, because if he had been thrown out of the car, it would have crushed him. He opened one eye, looked up at me, and reached up. He grabbed me by my suit and pulled me close.

"Don't let them touch me," he said, referring to the medics. "I don't want any of these guys touching me."

I said, "Nobody's going to touch you. Are you hurt anywhere?"

He said, "I don't think I'm hurt anywhere except my own mentality."

I came out of the ditch. The other guys started toward Walter, and I stopped them. "Let him get up on his own," I said. "Don't touch him, he'll get up."

A few minutes later, he did get up and walked slowly out of the ditch. He was embarrassed and, I know, hating himself for not listening to good advice. Walter was that way. If he thought he had made a mistake, he wanted to punish himself for it.

Another time, we were making some practice runs for a race in Detroit on the new course at Belle Isle. The track was difficult and narrow. He had made several laps, and the car was well heated up, but he got too close to the wall and clipped it. He knocked the spoiler off and did some other cosmetic damage, but the car was still running.

He pulled into the pits, and he just sat in the car. The crew chief came over to me and said, "Walter won't get out of the car."

"Just leave him there," I said. It was about 150 degrees inside the car, and I knew Walter was punishing himself for his mistake. "Don't force him, leave him alone and he will eventually get out of the car," I told the crew chief. He did, and we went back to the hotel and showered. We got cleaned up and went out to dinner as if nothing had happened.

When it came to athletics and training, Walter drove himself very hard. He was a perfectionist in everything he did, and nobody had to tell him when he made a mistake. He knew it, and nobody was harder on himself for making a mistake than Walter. I was honored that we became good friends and that he later joined our efforts to bring an NFL expansion team to St. Louis.

Walter was with me in Watkins Glen, New York, a few years later when it was his turn to make sure I was OK following an accident.

Rain had delayed the race. When that happens the grid often gets scrambled, shuffling some of the slower guys up front and the faster guys in the back. There were two guys in front of me I knew I could beat if I just went into, and out of, the last turn hard, which was what I did.

As I came out of the turn, however, one of the cars bumped the second car, and that knocked the second car into me as I passed on the left. It clipped my right rear quarter panel, turning me sideways and sending me straight into the concrete wall. The onboard computer said I hit the wall head-on at 155 miles an hour.

The car just exploded. The hood went thirty feet into the air and came floating down. When the car finally stopped spinning, Walter jumped over the five-foot concrete pit wall and got to the car to see if I was all right.

I vaguely remember saying, "Watch out for my neck," as he and others took the steering wheel off the car and pulled me out through the window. Walter said later he was talking to me and asking if I was OK, but I don't recall the conversation.

They took me to the first-aid station, and it just so happened that another wreck had happened on the track at almost the same moment I had crashed. The workers were attending to the other driver, and one of my crew members was at my side holding my helmet.

"I'm going to go with you to the hospital," he said. I really had no idea what he was talking about. I saw that he was holding my helmet but didn't know what had happened.

I sat down on a cot in the first-aid room and noticed a map of a racetrack on the wall. I looked at my suit and said, "I must be racing." Then I looked again at the map. Underneath, it said "Watkins Glen."

"I must be racing at Watkins Glen," I thought.

The nurse came in with her clipboard and started to take down information. She asked if I knew where I was. "Watkins Glen," I replied. She said, "Oh, you weren't dinged up too bad, what's your name?"

"Watkins Glen," I said.

"Oh, we do have a problem," she said. "We'd better get you over to the hospital."

I had a concussion, but they released me from the hospital and I went back to the motor coach and got ready to fly back to St. Louis. It was normal for some of the other drivers to come by after a race and have a cold Budweiser to relax a little before we all headed home. Some of the people who came by didn't realize I had been involved in a wreck.

One of the other drivers was Jack Baldwin from Marietta, Georgia. We laughed and drank a beer, and then we both left to head home. Later that night, watching ESPN, he saw my crash and called me on the telephone.

"When did you have that crash?" he said.

I told him it was right at the end of the race.

"But you were standing there with me drinking a beer," Baldwin said. "That car was demolished. How do you feel?"

"I feel like I got hit by a truck," I said.

It was a few days later when I actually saw the film of the wreck. ESPN had made it their "Crash of the Week," a dubious honor to be sure, and showed it over and over again. I was glad I had called my mother on the phone after the wreck to tell her she was most likely going to see it but that I was OK. It almost became embarrassing, because it replayed so many times.

One of my retail customers, Krieger's Sports Bar, actually wanted the hood of the car, so I signed and dated it and gave it to them. I think it still hangs in the restaurant.

I had other crashes, and near misses, and I still have pain caused from the accidents. I experienced a lot of severe headaches, because I cracked the fourth vertebra in my neck, and I have never regained the feeling in my little finger. It is just numb. I just take my pain medicine and don't think about it.

The hardest part of competing in racing at that level, in addition to being older than most of the drivers, was trying to do it on a part-time basis. I would work during the week at Grey Eagle, try to fly to wherever the race was on Thursday night so I could practice on Friday and qualify on Saturday, then race on Sunday. I was competing against drivers whose only job was to drive their racecar. Several of the drivers we competed against later raced in the Indianapolis 500 and the other major events.

I felt I was cheating myself out of seat time, because of all the other business commitments, and I just could not find the hours in the day or days in the week to devote more time to racing. I knew I had to give it up when I was going to a race in Dallas. Because of meetings, I could not get to the race until Sunday morning.

The officials let me drive the pace car around the track a few times so I could get a feel for the track, but I had to start at the rear. Midway through the race, somebody hit the wall in front of me, and lost a tire. It struck my car and broke the radiator. It was the last race of the season, and since I had announced that it would be my last, they honored me at the end-of-season banquet.

At that time, ESPN still televised most of the races on a delayed basis, at all times of the day and night. I told the crowd at the banquet that I was going to miss them but that if I missed them too much, I would simply set my video recorder to record the race at 3 a.m. and watch it later.

I really never looked back, because I knew I was too busy to keep racing.

In those days, racing was still more popular in the South

than in other parts of the country. One of the people trying to grow the sport nationally was Jim Trueman, who owned Bobby Rahal's car and the Red Roof hotel chain. He lived in Columbus, Ohio, and owned a track nearby—the Mid-Ohio Raceway at Mansfield, Ohio.

He called one day when I happened to be in Columbus, and we got together for a meeting. He said he was interested in building a new track for NASCAR racing, and he was considering locations in Fort Worth, Texas, or St. Louis. The area he had picked out in St. Louis was Riverport, in the northwest part of the county.

Trueman said he was having difficulty communicating with the proper personnel in St. Louis County and asked for my help. I made some phone calls but also got nowhere. I later found out it was because some of the people in the county government, including the county executive, Gene McNary, wanted to hold onto that site for a possible new football stadium. Jim then moved his attention to a location he had found in St. Charles County, but there was a dispute between St. Charles and St. Peters about city boundaries. It looked as if the site might get tied up in litigation.

I was at a race in Elkhart Lake, Wisconsin, when Jim came to my motor coach and asked to speak to me privately. He told me he had cancer and that his treatments were not going well, so he was dropping the project of building a new track. He was very sick, but he lived long enough to see Rahal, his driver, win the Indianapolis 500 the next year in his Budweiser car. Jim died eleven days after the race.

I have often wondered what economic benefits would have come to St. Louis if Jim had succeeded in his efforts to build the NASCAR track. It wasn't something I could take on, however. I was now fully involved in a battle myself.

The football Cardinals had left St. Louis for Phoenix, and we were trying to bring the NFL back to St. Louis.

The Clintons visit the St. Louis Riverfront, 1943. Grandfather Robert Clinton laid the "pavers" when the area was constructed.

Sitting between my sister Betty and brother Russ in Graniteville, the summer of 1942.

My birthplace in Graniteville, Missouri, 1937.

The Sheahan Company Store, Graniteville, Missouri, as it stands today.

The granite quarry, Graniteville, Missouri, as it looks today.

The huge granite stones are still cut into slabs and shipped all over the world.

Dino Colbichinni of Chicago and me doing our duty, 1959.

I am welcoming Mr. and Mrs. August Busch III and family, arriving at Eagle Estate, Warren County, Missouri, for Grey Eagle's 25th anniversary.

Lee and Mike Roarty greet August Busch III.

Jack Buck and I at one of the many charity luncheons we attended.

Jack Buck CF Golf Classic, 1974. From left you can locate Jimmy Hart, Dan Dierdorf, Willie Mays, Jay Randolph, Roger Maris, Mike Shannon, Mike Lieut, and me.

Time out for marlin fishing in the Bahamas. From left: Steve Jones, Tom Burnham, Tom Burrows, me, Tom Brahaney, and Al Hrabosky.

Yes, we caught a few!

The Busch Bison: former Cardinal Terry Stieve to left of Buffalo, Dan Dierdorf to right, Jim Hart to the right of Dan. I am front center, and Steve Jones is second from the right.

Former world champions Tommy Hearns and George Foreman take time out to say hello at a St. Louis boxing event.

I am in car #65, racing the Twelve Hours of Sebring race in Florida. We finished fourth in class.

At the Pro-Trans Am race in St. Petersburg, Florida.

Paul Newman and I at Road Atlanta. On a warm day, the interior of the car reaches more than 150°. If we look hot—we are!

Paul Newman and I at Paul's home track, Limerock, Connecticut (I used to call it "Slime" rock).

Stan Barrett, Hal Needham, me, and Paul Newman,
Bonneville Salt Flats, Utah. (Is that a cold Bud in
Paul's hand?!)

Gen. Chuck Yaeger, me, and Stan Barrett at Edwards
Air Force Base after Stan's historic run.

The Budweiser Rocket Car at top speed—739.666 mph. Rogers dried lake, California, December 17, 1979.

Paul Newman and me on the set of *Harry and Son*, Lake Worth, Florida.

Administrative office entrance, Grey Eagle Distributors, Inc.

Chapter 6

IT WAS IN THE FALL of 1987, after Bill Bidwill had announced that he was going to move the Cardinals from St. Louis to Phoenix after the season, when I received a phone call from my attorney, Walter Metcalfe. The mayor of St. Louis, Vince Schoemehl, wanted to meet with me.

I had no idea what Schoemehl wanted to talk to me about. We had been both business and social friends for years, dating back to his days as an alderman. One of his businesses had involved publishing newspapers targeted toward apartment residents in St. Louis County, where he also ran a sports league for the residents. He was a good salesman, and he talked Grey Eagle into becoming a sponsor of the league. The sponsorship cost $10,000 a year, at a time when we really were not spending that kind of money, but Vince convinced us it would benefit our business, and he was right.

I found out that Vince had become acquainted with a gentleman named Fran Murray. They previously had dinner together at a restaurant called Flutie's in New York. Murray was one of the owners. I had never met Fran or heard of him before Vince and Walter Metcalfe brought him into my office and said they wanted me to listen to his story.

It turned out Fran had an option to buy the New England Patriots. He was from Philadelphia and, I found out later, was a graduate of the Wharton School of Business. He was an interesting guy with a lot of ideas and plans. It turned out that for ten dollars, Schoemehl had purchased an option on Murray's option to buy the Patriots. Vince was thinking that a group of investors could come together and buy the Patriots and move

77

them to St. Louis to replace the Cardinals. Schoemehl thought I could head up that investor group. He had been hurt by the Cardinals' decision to move to Phoenix, feeling it was a move which hurt the credibility of his city, and he was determined to replace them as fast as possible.

It turned out that Schoemehl and Metcalfe had met Murray through Carl Icahn, then the chairman of TWA. Metcalfe worked for Bryan Cave, St. Louis' largest law firm, and he and Schoemehl had been associates since the early 1980s when they worked together to consolidate several hospitals into the St. Louis Regional Medical Center.

Even though Schoemehl himself joked about his ten-dollar option, Metcalfe told the *Post-Dispatch* that "it was a fairly highly documented transaction, it was a legitimate transaction . . . it made some sense."

While I didn't know Murray, I knew Schoemehl and trusted Metcalfe, my lawyer for more than twenty years. The more I listened to their ideas about finding an NFL team to replace the Cardinals, the more interested I became, especially with the idea of trying to secure an expansion franchise. With the Cardinals leaving, St. Louis was the largest television market without an NFL club and was the home of Anheuser-Busch, which spends millions of dollars in advertising with the NFL each year. It also appeared likely that the NFL was preparing for another round of expansion within a few years.

The first thing I noticed about Murray were his shoes. They were brown, and he was wearing a blue pinstriped suit. I knew he had to be a smooth talker to get away with wearing that combination, and I guess he kind of reminded me of Harold Hill, the fast-talking musical instrument salesman in "The Music Man."

What Murray was selling was the idea of bringing football back to St. Louis. We all knew that there would be no new NFL team for St. Louis if we did not build a new stadium. One of the reasons Bidwill left was his frustration over not getting his own stadium. The football Cardinals shared Busch Stadium with the baseball team, and it was said that Bidwill felt he had been treated like a second-class citizen.

Two members of Civic Progress, a group of twenty-eight to thirty of the largest companies in the area, even went to a league meeting—ironically in Phoenix—to pledge support for Bidwill in St. Louis. The story I heard was that the two, Chuck Knight and Bill Cornelius, even disagreed on the level of support in front of the entire league.

Bidwill wanted his own stadium and training facility and thought the city should pay for it. When it became clear he was never going to get it, he received the league's permission to relocate.

Of course, he was promised a new stadium in Phoenix, and he got it—in the fall of 2006, eighteen years after he left St. Louis.

I can honestly say I had never thought for one minute about the possibility of becoming an NFL owner before those gentlemen walked into my office. I had been a fan of the Cardinals and a season-ticket holder for many years. I had developed good relationships with many of the players such as Dan Dierdorf, Jim Hart, Johnny Roland, Roger Wehrli, and many others, and with the coaches—Don Coryell and Jim Hanifan. There were many days when my sons Jeff and Brian and I sat in Section 222, freezing our tails off and cheering for the Big Red, even though they were probably losing to Dallas at the time. The boys would want to go home because they were cold, but I would always talk them into staying another quarter.

Like all fans, I was upset when Bidwill and the Cardinals left. I could tell the city was mourning the loss. What bothered me the most was it seemed like St. Louis was developing a loser's mentality when it came to professional sports. Years earlier the St. Louis Hawks, an NBA club, had moved to Atlanta. Years before that, the Browns had left and had become the Baltimore Orioles. The only major pro sports teams we had were the baseball Cardinals and the Blues. I thought the loss of the NFL was hurting St. Louis' image as a major sports city.

Still, I didn't think it was incumbent upon me to start a campaign to bring another NFL team to St. Louis. I was willing to listen to what Fran, Vince, and Walter had to say, however.

Vince knew I had many friends among both Republicans and Democrats in the state legislature in Jefferson City. I had been active in getting legislation passed that supported the beer industry, and we were constantly aware of what was going on in the House and Senate. Many of the new laws under debate would affect our business.

All of us agreed that the only way to pursue a team for St. Louis was to build a new stadium. We knew it would have to be funded through the state and local governments. The way that made the most sense to me was to build a domed stadium and attach it to what was then Cervantes Convention Center. In addition to using the stadium for football, you could also use the facility to host major trade shows and conventions. Those activities would provide major economic benefits to the St. Louis region, which was what inspired me the most about participating in the process.

What didn't thrill me was the potential cost to pass the legislation to fund the stadium. I asked Metcalfe to give me an estimate of how much money he thought we would need. His guess was about $2 million in legal fees alone, just to write the legislative bill. There would be another $2 million for Fleishman-Hillard for public-relations costs and fees, in addition to the cost of wooing the NFL with all of the necessary travel and entertainment. A huge risk was at hand.

I was not in a position to shoulder that kind of financial burden alone. I quickly learned that Murray didn't have any money—he had borrowed heavily to buy his option on the Patriots. If I had known then all of the information that came out later about Murray's financial condition, I might have told him goodbye and never thought about his idea again. I really thought, however, that before Metcalfe and Schoemehl had asked me to meet with him, they would have fully explored his background. I knew he had lost some money when his fast-food restaurant chain collapsed, but I thought he had overcome that. He was a creative guy with a lot of ideas; that's what he brought to the partnership.

Since Murray didn't have any money, and I didn't want to cover all of the expenses myself, I had to find other people willing to invest in the partnership, with the idea that we would first lobby the legislature to pass a law to build the stadium and then try to acquire team. What I decided to do was to sell shares in the partnership for $250,000 each. I thought if we could get ten investors, we would have $2.5 million to work with—enough to cover the estimated legal costs, etc., to get the legislation passed.

I sent out thirty invitations to business leaders in the metro area. I was turned down twenty-nine times. The almost-universal opinion was that we had no chance for success, that it would be impossible to get the state, city, and county to agree on a project of this magnitude. These people had the money, but they considered the risk too great. The only person who stepped up and agreed to become an investor was Tom Holley, who owned the Grandpa's discount store chain.

Actually, one other group said yes, a family named Chomeau that ran an insurance business. They were enthusiastic at first but later found out that the company operated out of a trust and that the bylaws of the trust prohibited them from taking those kinds of entrepreneurial risks, so they had to withdraw.

The reaction really surprised me. I knew we would not get everyone's support, but I thought I would get more. It really bothered me, and I realized there were a lot of well-heeled people in St. Louis who had the funds to invest but never wanted to use their money for anything at risk!

That left me with a major decision to make. The would-be investors doubted that we could get the project done, but I disagreed. Murray was a supreme optimist, but he could easily be optimistic because he wasn't putting money on the table.

Nonetheless, he was an energetic, hard worker and was essential to the project.

It was clear to me that if we would proceed, I would have to cover the financial burden by myself. I took a couple of days to think it over. The business was going well, my son Jeff was progressing in the business, and I didn't want to run up a lot of unnecessary debt. I also was sensitive to the fact that if I developed cash-flow problems and could not adequately market my product, the senior management at Anheuser-Busch would not look favorably on the situation.

One of the problems was that we didn't have much time to waste. Metcalfe had determined that we could get the stadium built using general purpose bonds issued by the state, but they had a sunset date and were rapidly approaching their expiration date. If we didn't act quickly, and get the legislation passed quickly, we could not use those bonds.

I have often wondered what would have happened if I had come back to Murray, Schoemehl, and Metcalfe and said, "No, I just can't assume this financial risk to help this community get a football team." I am almost certain we would never have built the domed stadium, which meant that we never would have brought another NFL team to town.

It's difficult to imagine downtown St. Louis today without the stadium, without an NFL team, and without all of the other improvements that have occurred since the stadium was built. I honestly believe that much of that wouldn't have happened if my answer had been no.

Instead, I said yes. I was ready to accept this huge challenge.

Chapter 7

ON FEBRUARY 28, 1989, FRAN Murray and I held a news conference at my company, Grey Eagle, to announce the formation of the NFL partnership. I was recovering from oral surgery, so Murray did most of the talking. Talking was one of the things that he did best.

Before going public, I met with Metcalfe and told him I had three conditions that had to be met before I would agree to take on this kind of financial risk and workload.

The first was that I wanted the first right of refusal on all of Murray's stock. The purpose of that was that I needed to know who all my partners were. I told Walter that I really didn't know much about Murray—I didn't know who he knew, and I didn't want him selling his shares of our partnership to somebody I thought was questionable or of unsavory character. The laws governing my beer business dictated no affiliation with convicted felons. We had agreed that Murray would hold 51 percent of the stock in the partnership, and I would control 49 percent—selling off smaller shares to the limited investors, when and if needed. Murray got the 51 percent because of his ownership position with the Patriots. We really thought it was our strongest asset toward getting an expansion team.

Secondly, I told Walter, "You have a better vision of this than I do. I don't want to get into this project for more money than I can afford. You are a director of my company; you know my earnings and expenses. You know what the bottom line is. I don't want to get involved where today it is going to cost me $10 and tomorrow it's going to be $10 million. If you see something like that coming we have to re-evaluate our position quickly."

The third condition, I said, was that I did not want to ever be put in a position where I was at odds with any public official. "I am selling a consumer product, and I have to protect and respect those relationships," I said.

Metcalfe agreed that all of those conditions seemed reasonable, so we scheduled the news conference and went public with our plan to bring the NFL back to St. Louis. The media filled the conference room and I came to the realization of the enormous impact this was having on our community. All I could think of was, "What have I got myself into?"

Then we went to work. Some of the tasks seemed insurmountable, and the days grew long.

What we knew to be difficult, on the state level, was to convince the legislators from Kansas City, Springfield, and the rest of the state to support a project which would bring the most direct economic benefit to the City of St. Louis and St. Louis County. In order to generate more support, we helped develop a bill that would also include financial assistance to rebuild the H. Roe Bartle Convention Center in Kansas City and a minor league baseball stadium in Springfield.

The other argument we made as the centerpiece of our proposal was called the "new net public fiscal benefit." This was basically a government model that showed for every dollar spent by people visiting our city for events at the domed stadium, that dollar would be turned over 2 ½ times in taxable revenue to the city and state. People coming to the convention center/stadium for football games, trade shows, conventions, concerts, etc., would be spending money on tickets, lodging, food, transportation, and other items. These expenditures are taxed at the first spending level. The business that receives the revenue uses the income to purchase food, clothes, transportation, etc. This spending is taxed again at the second spending level. Therefore, the taxation from the original spending can be tracked two and a half times. The taxable benefit to the city would be tremendous.

The benefit to the rest of the state was in the tax dollars that would be flowing into the state's general revenue fund, which meant those dollars could be dolled out around the state. This was essential to gain the support of the outstate legislators. The plan was for the state to own half of the domed stadium facility, the City of St. Louis 25 percent, and St. Louis County 25 percent. Of course, the county benefit would be the overflow usage of restaurant and lodging facilities.

Time was working against us. We had less than three months left in the legislative session, and if the bill was not passed and signed into law in time, we would not be able to use tax-free bonds that would expire if not purchased soon.

On our first trip to Jefferson City we met with a state official about drafting the finance legislation. He asked us what we were doing, and we told him we wanted to build a stadium.

He said, "You fools. Don't you realize you can't just walk in down here and start talking to people and get legislative support? You need a lobbyist." We said, "OK, tell us what to do, and we'll do it." Then we went out and hired two lobbyists.

The legislation was submitted on the last possible day it could have been submitted. Thankfully, we had a lot of friends who worked hard on our behalf, people like state senators John Scott, Jet Banks, and Jim Mathewson of Sedalia, who was the president pro tem of the Senate. Tony Ribaudo from the House was on our side from the beginning. Ronnie DePasco from Kansas City also came on board with us pretty quickly when we added the Kansas City and Springfield projects. Many nights we dragged ourselves out of the governor's office at midnight, wondering if the deal was going to get done.

The bill passed both the House and Senate on May 14, just hours before the legislature went into summer recess. Then we had to wait two months for Governor Ashcroft to decide whether he was going to sign or veto the bill. He waited until the last possible day, two months later, to sign it, or he would have been required by law to veto it. Getting the word that he had signed the bill into law prompted our first mini-celebration.

Next, we had to turn our attention to the local governments in the City of St. Louis and St. Louis County. We were able to get an agreement more easily in the city, which obviously stood to gain the most direct revenue from the project. Tom Villa, a good friend, was president of the Board of Aldermen and an early supporter of the project. The county proved more difficult. Their portion of the debt service was approximately $5 million a year. A 3 ½ percent increase in the hotel-motel tax would provide this revenue. Our partnership called a meeting with the hotel-motel association to ask for their support of this additional tax. They agreed, knowing this would bring them to about the same rate as the city hotels and motels. Their gain would be the additional revenue from the overflow business from the city. The measure passed with an approval rate of more than 70 percent. The county was now on board.

I learned a lot about politics and how deals get done during this process. Gene McNary had resigned as the St. Louis County Executive to take a job in the federal government as the head of the Immigration and Naturalization Service, so H. C. Milford was serving as the interim executive until the next election. I always knew the city and county governments were at odds on most issues, but I never realized how much animosity and jealousy there were between the two entities until I got involved in this deal.

Most of my meetings with Milford came late at night, and at one point he told me that in order to give his support to this project he really needed to get more representation on the Airport Board. Lambert Field, the St. Louis airport, is owned and operated by the City of St. Louis but is located in St. Louis County. The Airport Board consists of representatives from both the city and the county.

I left that meeting and went to Schoemehl and said, "Vince, Milford needs more support. You have to agree to give him a couple more seats on the Airport Board."

"We can do that," Schoemehl said. "We'll increase the size of the board by four seats and he can have two of them." Therefore, the city maintained a comfortable majority.

Another time, Milford told me he needed more of a voice on the Bi-State Development Agency, the company that runs the transit system in the city, county, and Illinois. I relayed that message to Schoemehl and this time his response was, "Tell H. not to be pushing too hard too fast."

Those were the kind of negotiations I had to go through. It was more than I had ever bargained for, and at times it made me feel as if I wanted to pull my hair out.

Virvus Jones was the comptroller of the City of St. Louis, and he was totally against the project. He tried to block our efforts every chance he got. He made public statements that he thought Murray and I were crooks. Schoemehl would tell him to do something and he would totally ignore him. A couple of years into the deal he was supposed to cut a check for $500,000 to pay the stadium architect, HOK Sport, for the work they had done so far and he refused to write the check, even when Schoemehl told him to do it. Finally, I had to write the check or HOK would have been forced to pull its people from the job, backing up the project and delaying the completion of the stadium in time for the start of the 1995 season. This was one of the many things I had to do in order to keep the project moving forward.

Jones wanted a special tax to be used to fund the city's cost of the stadium, a move that would require a vote by city residents, causing another delay. Luckily, the mayor and Board of Aldermen ignored his idea.

In addition to getting all three governmental bodies to agree on the terms for the construction of the stadium, I had to get them to agree on the terms of the lease. The lease was very important to me, because it was the only guarantee I had of getting the money back that I had invested in the legislative effort to get the stadium built. Since the stadium was going to be owned by the state, city, and county, the lease was the only thing of value that encouraged me to continue.

Technically, the lease belonged to the NFL partnership, which at the time consisted of myself, Murray, and my old racing buddy, Walter Payton. Murray had a 70 percent stake in the lease and I had a 30 percent stake. Murray had agreed to give Walter 10 percent of his share of the lease in order for him to join our group. We all thought having an NFL icon like Walter in our group would dramatically enhance our chances with the league.

When we completed the negotiations with all of the governmental bodies, I had no idea the lease would turn out to be such a big issue in the months and years to come.

Payton kept me laughing on a lot of the tough days, and he also was there the night we celebrated passing the hotel-motel tax, the final piece to getting the county government's approval. He had campaigned for the tax, even though he previously had an operation on his foot. While I was doing a television interview, he came up behind me and whacked me on the backside with his cane. I knew immediately who had done it.

I reciprocated by coming up to him while he was being interviewed and knocking his cane out from under him, causing him to drop sharply to one side. Those fun times made the tough days easier to take.

Our third partner, Murray, was an interesting individual. As I learned more about his background, I found out he ran a company that had divergent businesses operating in six states—he was in the health care industry in New Jersey, the publishing business in Texas, restaurants in New York, and cattle and equipment sales in Georgia. I found out he had been a wheeler-and-dealer ever since he was a young boy, when he sold sodas and hot dogs at weekly bingo games in his neighborhood.

He also had real estate holdings, a few racehorses, and of course, his investment in the Patriots.

Murray's brother Jim was a football guy, having been involved with the Philadelphia Eagles for years, including a stint as the team's general manager. Murray had gotten involved with the Patriots when his company loaned Billy Sullivan, at the time the owner of the Patriots, $21 million when Sullivan was strapped for cash. I later learned much of the Patriots' financial problems occurred as a result of investing in Don King and Michael Jackson's world tour. I am not kidding.

King was promoting Jackson's world tour, and he wanted to stage a concert at Foxboro Stadium, where the Patriots played. He met with Chuck Sullivan, Billy's son, and by the time that meeting was over there was not only going to be a concert in Foxboro but the Sullivans had also agreed to invest in the world-wide tour.

The world tour was a financial disaster and cost the Sullivans a lot of money, which affected their football operation. That's when Murray came along and loaned the Sullivans his borrowed money in exchange for a three-year option to buy the Patriots and Foxboro Stadium.

It took all three years and involved a lot of complicated financial activity. At one point Murray thought he had settled with the Sullivans by agreeing to buy the Patriots. Instead, the Sullivans sold 51 percent of the team to Victor Kiam, the owner of the Remington Corp., leaving Murray with 49 percent ownership in the team as repayment for the loan he had given the Sullivans.

Even though Murray now owned 49 percent of an NFL team, a share that was later valued at $38 million, he still had no actual money. All of that money was in stock. I was putting the money into the NFL partnership, and he was taking draws in order to cover his living expenses. I also was paying for all of his and my expenses, as well as our entourage of lawyers and PR people, and for travel around the country to wine and dine the NFL officials and owners. I later determined that I loaned him about $3 million over the course of our business relationship. However, this, I was told, was necessary to keep him available and focused on the project.

The leverage Murray had was his minority ownership of the Patriots and his connections and access to the other NFL owners. He always assured me that if we were successful in bringing an NFL franchise to St. Louis, he would sell his share of the Patriots and become the majority owner of our new team. I took him at his word.

I also took Fran at his word that his past money problems were behind him. I knew he would have had to have passed scrutiny by the NFL and the other owners before they would have approved the sale of the Patriots, but it still made me a little uneasy when KMOX Radio reported in December 1989 that Murray had been successfully sued at least twenty-two times in Pennsylvania and New York for failing to pay debts.

The station also reported it had learned that various local, state, and the federal governments had filed eleven tax-related suits against Murray. All of those cases, I was later told, stemmed from the collapse of Murray's chain of fast-food restaurants. He blamed their collapse on the gasoline crisis of the mid-1970s.

I had to support Fran publicly because I was afraid of the negative repercussions those allegations would have on our efforts not only to get the stadium built but also to acquire the expansion team. I also thought I still needed his help, along with Payton, if we were going to be successful in our efforts.

What I soon found out, however, is that while Murray was working with me, he also had some other secret negotiations going on. That was when James Orthwein came on the scene.

Chapter 8

THERE MIGHT NEVER HAVE BEEN a more unlikely pair to become business partners than myself and Jim Orthwein. The biggest problem I had was that I didn't know he and I were going to become partners until it was already a done deal, and I had no say in the matter.

Usually when you agree to go into business with someone you at least have a chance to say yes or no. I felt that Murray and Metcalfe never gave me that chance, and in reality, this was the beginning of the end of our hopes to acquire an expansion franchise.

Orthwein was born into the Busch family. His mother, Clara, was August Busch Jr.'s sister, making him August III's cousin. At the time, it was reported that he owned about 1.3 million shares of stock in Anheuser-Busch and sat on the company's board of directors. That stock had a street value of about $56 million. The only director who owned more stock was August III.

While I had spent many days as a young boy eating only a bread-and-butter sandwich for lunch because our family didn't have enough money to buy lunchmeat, Orthwein was riding horses and learning to be a competitive sailor. At his prep school, he was captain of the skeet-shooting team.

For thirty-six years, Orthwein was in the advertising business. From 1976 to 1983, he served as chairman of D'Arcy-MacManus & Masius, one of the largest agencies in the world because it handled many of the brewery's accounts. He was now working as the chairman of Huntleigh Asset Partners, a private investment firm in Clayton. He also had other investment companies as well, and was a partner in a yacht building and repair business in Florida.

The link between myself and Orthwein was Walter Metcalfe, who also had been Orthwein's attorney for more than ten years.

Murray apparently had begun telling Metcalfe about all of his financial problems. He knew he could not ask me for more money, plus I did not have the resources to bail him out of his problems with the Patriots. I'm certain that Metcalfe knew Orthwein had that kind of money.

Murray later told me that their meetings took place at the old Busch's Grove restaurant without me. It's my understanding that in those meetings, an agreement was reached for Orthwein to loan Murray $15 million, in exchange for Murray giving Orthwein 12 percent of the NFL partnership. The loan was to be repaid from the revenues generated by our new team.

Eventually, Orthwein increased the loan to $30 million. Murray agreed to put up his 49 percent ownership of the Patriots as collateral. I believe Metcalfe drafted the agreement, and all sides agreed that it would remain confidential.

I don't know when they planned to tell me, but I quickly learned of the change in our partnership and called Metcalfe to try to find out what was going on.

"Walter, how did this happen?" I said. "I thought we had an understanding that I would have first rights on all of Murray's stock. I didn't know about any meetings at Busch's Grove. I wasn't invited, and apparently stock has changed hands here."

Metcalfe said, "Jerry, I thought I was operating in your best interests. Jim Orthwein carries the Busch name. It's an important name for the NFL. He has the capital to do the things that need to be done with this partnership. I thought it was best that we work an agreement to solve more than one problem."

I told Metcalfe, "Walter, that may be true, but you never did put the question before me. That's what I am really disappointed about."

Part of the problem was that while it had been widely known that I was looking for investors, I never heard from Jim Orthwein. Metcalfe knew I needed investors, and he never told me that Orthwein was interested. Then, when all of the risk was removed, the money had been spent to get the legislation passed and the lease agreements signed, and we were ready to issue the bonds and begin construction of the stadium, he suddenly showed up.

I really didn't blame Orthwein. He was a businessman and was presented with a deal that nobody in their right mind would refuse. In my mind, it came down to either representing Orthwein with his mega-bucks, or me. It seemed to me that Metcalfe chose the money over a higher degree of ethics. I was disappointed and angry.

Another part of the problem was that everybody involved was being very vague on the terms of the deal between Orthwein and Murray. Murray said it was only a temporary arrangement, and that as soon as his financial picture improved he would be rejoining the St. Louis partnership. Orthwein and Metcalfe both said Murray had to meet "certain conditions" before he could rejoin our partnership, but I never did learn what those conditions were—I guess because Murray never met them.

There also was confusion over what was going on with the Patriots.

In the fall of 1991, Victor Kiam's deadline to buy Murray's stake of the team expired because he didn't have the money. Orthwein, trying to protect his investment—the loan to Murray—decided to buy out Kiam's share of the team. A few months later, Orthwein foreclosed on his loan to Murray, taking his share of the Patriots as the collateral he had put up on the loan. That made Orthwein the 99 percent owner of the Patriots, with his associate, Michael O'Halloran, owning the remaining 1 percent.

Orthwein, apparently also as part of his agreement with

Murray, took over Murray's role as head of our NFL partnership, in effect making him my boss.

I probably would not have been happy having Orthwein as a minority investor, but I certainly didn't like having him in charge—after all of the time, effort, and money I had put into the deal.

Plus, I was confused by how the whole deal had transpired, even after I tried to piece it together after the fact. I wondered how Orthwein could own one team and be trying to get another team for St. Louis. That didn't seem to make much sense, and I knew there was increasing talk around the league that if we were not awarded an expansion team, Orthwein could simply move the Patriots to St. Louis. It was a very confusing time.

I knew if I was confused about what was going on—and I was one of the main people involved—others around the NFL would be confused too. We had to be 100 percent unified or we would have no hope of landing an expansion team. We had to clear up that confusion.

The best way to do that, I thought, was to get Orthwein and Murray together and just talk through all of the issues and everything that had transpired. I didn't want there to be any distractions so I suggested we meet in Fort Lauderdale, Florida, where Jim has a home. It was a very tense and sensitive situation.

I docked my boat behind Jim's house in the bay, and we actually met on the boat. Before we began, I said, "We are going to keep this as business-like as possible. I am going to set down a few rules before we start."

I told both Orthwein and Murray, "I don't want any swearing or personal name-calling. There will be no consumption of alcohol until this meeting is over. We need to take the personalities out of it and be as direct with the issues as we can possibly be." Both agreed with those rules, so we began to talk.

We met until the middle of the afternoon, then decided to knock off for the day. We were inside Jim's house, getting ready to leave for dinner, when the telephone rang. I could tell from what Jim was saying that it was August Busch III. From what Jim was saying, it appeared August was asking him what his intentions were with the Patriots.

August apparently was reminding him that if he moved the Patriots out of New England, he would be losing a great deal of market share for Anheuser-Busch products in that part of the country. Customers from throughout New England would no doubt retaliate against the move of the team by boycotting Anheuser-Busch beer. That would, of course, be very destructive to the company's marketing plan in that region.

I recall Jim being a little obstinate and saying something to the effect that August "should be more interested about the wholesalers in that area imposing a twenty-case delivery minimum to their retail customers." The conversation seemed to get a little strained at that point, and Jim eventually slammed the phone down and said, "Nobody is going to tell me how I am going to spend my money."

I knew then that the Patriots would never, ever be moving to St. Louis.

Despite my best intentions, none of our issues were resolved. We were continuing our efforts toward the expansion process, and Jim called a meeting one afternoon at his office in Clayton. The meeting included myself, Payton, Metcalfe, and Michael O'Halloran, who works for Orthwein.

Since Orthwein had assumed Murray's role in the partnership, he really was in control. I didn't like it, and I didn't agree with it—primarily because of the way the change had come about, and the fact that Jim and I had different ideas about what needed to be done and how to go about running our business. I was always a hands-on owner, believing it was the best way to keep a business running smoothly, and I felt Orthwein was much more willing to delegate authority and responsibility and not be involved in the day-to-day decisions.

Because Jim was in control, I was mostly listening during the meeting until he said, "Under our reorganized partnership we are going to have a different way of voting on the issues. Regardless of the amount of stock you have you will get one vote."

I said, "Jim that is going to leave us with an opportunity to be deadlocked, two-two. Four of us have stock in the partnership (myself, Orthwein, Payton, and Michael O'Halloran, who had 2 percent)."

Orthwein said, "No, there are five of us. Walter (Metcalfe) has stock."

I was stunned. This was another new development over which I had never been consulted or agreed to.

I looked at Walter and said, "Walter, do you have stock in this partnership?"

He said, "I have 1 percent."

"Where did you get that 1 percent?" I said. "Did it roll off the table and you picked it up? I'd like to know. I had the rights of first refusal on all stock. How did this come about?"

Orthwein answered, "Walter has given us very important pro bono work on this project."

"Pro bono work my foot," I said, or something to that effect. "I've paid his firm more than $2 million according to my books. This isn't pro bono to me."

Payton had sat quietly during these exchanges, but finally he looked at me and said, "Jerry, what is going on?"

"Walter, you and I just got aced out of any voice in this partnership," I said.

Payton stood up and walked over to the telephone and called Bud Holmes in Louisiana, who had been Payton's agent during his playing career and still ran all of his financial affairs. Payton told him about the changes in our partnership, and Holmes said he would be in touch with Metcalfe to try to find out what was going on. I don't know if they ever met or not.

All I did know was that I was being squeezed between a rock and a hard place. Orthwein didn't care about bringing a football team to St. Louis. He already owned the Patriots, and it seemed all he cared about that deal was that he knew he would be able to sell the team and make a nice profit, which is exactly what he did. But because he technically was in charge of the partnership, there really was very little I could do. Since he wasn't going to be our primary investor, I still needed that person to be able to put this deal together, but I had nothing to offer them in exchange except portions of my part of the stock, which was not enough for that kind of investment.

The press finally started getting wind of the disagreements between Orthwein and myself. They tried to call it a fight between old money and new money, which was bunk. The *Post-Dispatch* did everything it could to try to throw a monkey wrench into what we were trying to accomplish. They certainly didn't help anything.

One of our disagreements came when Walter Payton was elected into the Pro Football Hall of Fame. I thought it would enhance our position with the league if our partnership paid for a congratulatory full-page ad in *USA Today*. Orthwein didn't want to do it, so I took out the ad and paid for it myself.

We also disagreed on whether we should advertise as part of our premium-seat sales campaign, and basically we just had a different managerial style.

I knew from conversations with a variety of NFL people over the years that St. Louis was the preferred site for one of the two new expansion franchises. But I also was enough of a businessman to know that the league did not want to get involved with a group that was filled with in-fighting, which was exactly the case with our group. I really didn't know what to do, so I actually sought the advice of the NFL commissioner, Paul Tagliabue.

My new attorney, Jim Shoemake, and I met with Tagliabue and Neil Austrian, the president of the NFL, one day at the league offices in New York.

"I'm really in a situation here where I am not sure where to go," I said. "How am I going to get a team for St. Louis out of this?"

Tagliabue and the others, I thought, were very honest and direct in their comments. They basically told me what the feelings were around their offices and the NFL for Orthwein and Metcalfe, and their opinions did not change my belief that we were fighting an uphill battle.

I left that meeting convinced that there was only one thing to do. I had to buy Orthwein out of his share of the partnership and then look for a new majority owner.

My only other option was to challenge the deal between Murray and Orthwein in court, arguing that Orthwein had obtained Murray's stock illegally—because of my position of having the right of first refusal on all stock transactions.

I have no doubt I would have prevailed in court, but how long that would have taken—and what effect the effort would have had on our pursuit of a team—was the question that I couldn't answer. I could not afford to take that risk.

I really felt terribly betrayed by both Murray and Metcalfe. It was my feeling that they didn't go about the deal the right way. My feeling was that if both had displayed a lot more personal business ethics, then everything would have worked out for everyone concerned.

Murray had to get money, I soon realized that. He was in far worse financial shape than I ever realized when I found out that many of his bills in St. Louis were not being paid. More people were filing lawsuits against Murray because of unpaid debts. Between 1990 and 1993, the *Post-Dispatch* reported that he had run up another $3 million in debts. He was facing foreclosure on homes in Pennsylvania and New Jersey, and he was being sued for non-payment of loans on restaurants and nursing homes.

I asked Murray several times what had happened and all he did was tap dance around the issues. I never got a straight answer from him. He spoke in riddles.

Murray told the *Post-Dispatch* that the list of judgments was not "a pattern of voluntary non-payment. It's a pattern of extraordinary disadvantage I've suffered. . . . I was getting killed during this whole period in my pursuit of this franchise."

Metcalfe had also become very vague and distant. I didn't talk to Metcalfe for more than a month when he finally called me early in 1993.

"There are two ways to do this and get past this issue," I told Metcalfe. "Either Orthwein dissolves his shares because I don't think he had a right to them anyway, or I will buy them away from him. He can keep the Patriots and sell them at his leisure."

I told Metcalfe that we really were at a stalemate unless I was able to buy Orthwein out, because nothing was being accomplished. We were not moving forward in our efforts to obtain a team. Orthwein wanted total autonomy, and that's not the way a partnership works.

Metcalfe agreed to relay my offer to Orthwein, but then he stepped out of the deal, obviously because it was getting publicized that there were areas of personal conflict for him. I started dealing with a personal injury lawyer named Jim Koester, who was negotiating with me for Orthwein.

Even though I was the one who had put up all the money and taken all of the risk, Orthwein said he wanted to be "compensated" for his work in the partnership. I think the final price came to something like $2.8 million. I went to Koester's office in Clayton late one night and gave him the check. Orthwein wasn't there, but Koester relayed the news that I had turned over the check.

The newspaper started criticizing me again, even though they did not know very much of what was actually going on. I knew there was no way the Patriots were ever going to move to St. Louis, but I couldn't say that. They didn't know that Orthwein told me that he was not going to spend any more money to try to bring a team to St. Louis. I couldn't say that. It was becoming obvious the press did not want to support my position.

Part of my agreement with Orthwein was that if we did not obtain an expansion team, he would control 65 percent of the stadium lease, I would control 30 percent, Tom Holley had 4 percent, and Metcalfe still had his 1 percent. Our lease gave us up to two years to try to bring another team to St. Louis if we did not receive an expansion franchise, a protection I had fought for very hard since there were no guarantees about the expansion process.

I learned that lesson the hard way.

Chapter 9

IN MAY 1991, THE NFL made the announcement we had anticipated—the league planned to add two new expansion teams. No specific timetable was set, but we were encouraged and believed our chances were as good as any other hopeful.

That summer, we completed the negotiations for the NFL partnership to lease the new domed stadium for our team's home games, another important step in our effort. At the time, there were some labor disagreements between the league and the players association, and the possibility of a delay of the expansion appeared. One key element we insisted on including in the lease agreement was that the agreement would remain in place for two years following the completion of the stadium's construction.

This was our protection. If for some reason the NFL decided not to expand, or if we were not awarded an expansion team, the lease gave our group an extra two years to try to persuade an existing NFL team to move to St. Louis.

Even though we felt confident about the expansion process, there was no guarantee. Too many variables were at stake to be able to say with 100 percent certainty that we would be awarded a team. At the time, we also did not know what the price was going to be for the team—our best guess was that it would be somewhere in the $80–85 million range.

What I did know to be a fact was that there were several existing NFL teams that were unhappy with their current situations. If we did not obtain an expansion franchise, I was reasonably confident we could persuade some other team—not the Patriots—to move to St. Louis. There were teams that were unhappy with their stadium lease, teams that did not like the fact that they were sharing a stadium with a baseball team, and teams that were unhappy with their local market support.

Some of the owners had spoken to me, not in specific terms, but in direct-enough language that I knew they were well aware of what was happening in St. Louis. One owner even walked up behind me at one of their meetings and stuck his business card in my coat pocket and said, "We may have to talk down the road somewhere." That was Bud Adams, who owned the Houston Oilers and soon thereafter moved his team to Nashville.

The lease was the only guarantee I had of getting the money back that I invested in the effort to bring an NFL team to St. Louis. It was never anything more than that. It was my insurance plan—otherwise, I would be spending millions of dollars with no assurances whatsoever.

On March 18, 1992, the NFL announced that four cities that had applied for an expansion team—Honolulu, Raleigh-Durham, Nashville, and San Antonio—had been dropped from consideration. Two months later, Oakland and Sacramento were told they were no longer expansion candidates. The finalists were Baltimore, Charlotte, Memphis, Jacksonville, and St. Louis.

The groundbreaking of the domed stadium was on a brutally hot July day in 1992. It was a very humbling experience and a realization of all my years of hard work. Here was a $260 million project that I had helped create, and it was being built only a few miles from the housing projects where I had grown up. As satisfying as that moment was, however, we knew our work was a long way from being completed.

The task at hand now was to raise money. We had to find investors who could join our group, including a majority owner. I already knew Jim Orthwein was not going to be that person, even though much of the St. Louis print media thought otherwise. I thought we needed to raise about $45 million, which would allow us to borrow the rest of what we thought was going to be the fee for the expansion team.

A group of owners formed the NFL finance committee, and they had a meeting in Chicago for all of the prospective expansion cities to present a report on their financial situations. We had one investor, from Pittsburgh, who was prepared to join our group, but he did not want his name revealed at this meeting or to the media. We asked the committee if we could keep his name private, and they agreed.

Buzz Westfall spoke on our behalf, and Tim Snavely, my tax accountant, made the formal financial presentation. During the question and answer session, one of the owners whom I didn't recognize asked me a direct question: "Was it always your desire to own an NFL franchise?"

That answer was easy—no—but I didn't want to come right out and say that for fear of making them feel I had less than 100 percent interest in ownership.

"Sir, let me answer you this way," I said. "I grew up as a very poor kid in the housing projects of St. Louis. I never dreamed I would own a major Anheuser-Busch wholesalership. I never dreamed beyond that. What I am doing here today is for the NFL fans of St. Louis. They deserve a franchise. It has always been a supportive NFL city."

I sat back down and he thanked me, and as I continued to watch him, he nudged his buddy sitting next to him. I felt like he was saying, "This is the kind of guy we're looking for." I saw a lot of smiles around the room, and everyone involved in our presentation was smiling as we left Chicago and headed home.

One of the biggest questions still not answered by the league was how much the expansion team was going to cost. Jerry Jones had bought the Dallas Cowboys for $140 million, but for that price he was buying an established team and some hard, physical assets. With an expansion team, all we were getting was the right to have a team—we would have all of the extra costs on top of the expansion fee.

We got the bad news in an Atlanta hotel in May 1993. The owners set the expansion fee at $140 million, far greater than we ever expected or anticipated. In addition, the owners said that the expansion teams also would receive only half of the league's television revenue for their first three seasons. In effect, that made the expansion fee a whopping $204 million.

Furthermore, the league said the first payment of $90 million had to be paid in cash up front before the team had played its first game. Jerry Jones later told me that he paid this same amount up front when he bought the Cowboys. We were nowhere close to that financial goal.

Walter Payton was at the meeting with me, and when we heard the news we just stared at each other in silence. Finally, I said, "Walter, there goes our hope and our dream. We might as well just go home."

We turned and started heading down the hallway, and suddenly somebody was calling my name, running after me, telling me to wait up. It was Jerry Jones.

He caught up to us, and we all sat down in some chairs in the hotel lobby. "Don't be discouraged by this," Jones said. "I had to pay $140 million for the Cowboys, with $90 million up front. There are ways you can cover the costs."

Jones then explained to me how he structured the Cowboys' finances so he could recoup all of that money. I told him we would consider all of those things, then Payton and I left and headed home.

I think it was more than a coincidence that the price of the expansion teams turned out to be exactly the same as the cost that Jones had paid for the Cowboys. The last time the NFL had expanded was in 1976, with a $16 million fee. Raising the fee to $140 million, not even including the loss of television revenue, marked an increase of 875 percent in only 17 years. The *Post-Dispatch* reported that if you had invested the same $16 million in the stock market in 1976, the value would have increased only 3.5 times.

We weren't the only potential ownership group that was shocked by the amount of the expansion fee. Unfortunately, there was nothing any of us could do about it—we either had to find a way to come up with the money or drop our bid for a team. The final alternative would be to make a deal with an existing team to relocate to St. Louis.

Our odds of getting a team were hurt even more when it was leaked to the press that my would-be lead investor was John Connelly, a businessman from Pittsburgh who owned the *Admiral,* a large entertainment boat on the St. Louis riverfront. We had known each other for several years. I had put together a nationally televised boxing match on the *Admiral* in 1986, trying to give some exposure to Arthur Jimmerson and Louis Howard, a couple of up-and-coming boxers from St. Louis.

It was called the Budweiser Rumble on the River, and the fights were televised by ESPN. The fights gave the boxers and the city some good national exposure. I had hoped to break even financially, but the deal didn't work out that well, and I ended up losing about $10,000.

I had talked Connelly into being the lead investor for our expansion bid, but the one condition he placed on his involvement was that he didn't want his name used until the deal was completed. He was afraid there would be bad publicity if it was known that he was involved, and somehow the deal fell through. I heard later the Rooney family—who owned the Steelers—were not friendly with Connelly.

I was at home one night when Vince Schoemehl showed up at my front door. Vince was no longer the mayor by this time and was working as some kind of a correspondent for KSDK-TV, the NBC affiliate in town. At almost the same time, my telephone rang. Connelly was calling me.

He didn't mince his words. "Jerry, I have to pull out of this deal," Connelly said. "Somebody, and I think I know who it was, leaked my name to the media. That was the one thing I asked; that I not be identified until the deal was completed." Then he really surprised me by asking if Schoemehl was there. When I said yes, he said, "Put him on."

Even though I was not on the phone, I could still hear Connelly. He ripped into Vince, convinced that Schoemehl had been the one who had announced that Connelly was going to be our lead investor.

If that had not happened, I am convinced Connelly would have remained in our group. Still, however, we were only about halfway toward raising the amount of money we needed before the expansion teams were scheduled to be awarded in October 1993—now just a few months away. It seemed ironic to me that one of the people who had talked me into this deal was the same person who may have cost me a lead investor.

That was when I came up with the idea of using the stadium lease as the collateral for a loan to cover the rest of our franchise fee.

It seemed like a good idea to me, but apparently not to anybody else. I really thought I could borrow the $50 million I needed by putting up the $900 million, 30-year lease as collateral. I called Drew Baur, the head of Southwest Bank, and ran the idea past him. He said he thought it sounded reasonable to him, but it would most likely take a consortium of banks. He said I should call the lead bank in town, which at the time was Boatmen's. So I picked up the phone and arranged a meeting.

Boatmen's turned its back on me. They wanted me to put up my company, Grey Eagle, as collateral for the loan. There was no way I could or would do that. Plus, I thought I had enough collateral by using the stadium lease. I had a $900 million lease, and I could not borrow $50 million. I only had to have the money if we got the team, and then the lease would have gone into effect. There was no way the deal could not work.

I was very disappointed, but I guess I shouldn't have been surprised—considering how little response I had received from the St. Louis business community when I was first trying to line up investors to join our group.

Rep. Richard Gephardt contacted me and asked if there

was anything he could do to help. "Well, if you know anybody with about $100 million they want to invest in an NFL team that would be nice," I said. He actually said he would put a list together and see if those people would talk to me.

The response was what I expected. One man was going through a divorce and was worried that if he got involved he would have to declare all of his financial holdings, which would affect the terms of his divorce. Most said they might be interested if it was in their town, but they couldn't see doing it to bring a team to St. Louis.

Eventually, I turned to August Busch III and presented all of the information to him. I told him I wanted to present him with an investment opportunity, and I thought it was a good one. He listened and even had Jerry Ritter, his executive vice president, look the deal over, but a few days later he called and turned me down. He said, "This just isn't my kind of deal. I don't invest that way." I understood that. I really would have been shocked had he said yes. I really believe that if August could have found an outside chance to be involved, he would have.

A day or so later he called back and asked me how I was doing. "I'm doing great August, if you could just come out here and get this gun out of my hand." He said, "Don't talk that way. It's not funny." Of course, I was joking!

It was no secret I was looking for a major investor. A friend of mine, Gus Otto, had played football at Missouri and then with the Oakland Raiders. He called me at home early one morning.

"Jerry, I don't know what I was thinking of," he said. "Last night my wife Sue and I were going through all the possibilities of people we knew who might be able to come in and help you. We both sat up in bed and looked at each other and said, 'Stan Kroenke.'"

I said, "Who is Stan Kroenke?"

Gus explained that Kroenke lived in Columbia and had married into the Walton family. He had made money on his own by building and developing shopping centers adjacent to Wal-

Mart stores all around the country. I didn't know him and had never heard of him.

Gus gave me Kroenke's phone number, and I made a couple of calls but never got a return call. Then I wrote him a letter and said I would like to meet with him, and that he could pretty much name his own terms for the deal as long as I was able to retain at least 10 percent of the team. Again I never received a response. It was as if I didn't exist or the letter didn't exist.

I was about to find out why.

Chapter *10*

JACK BUCK WAS BROADCASTING A Monday night game for CBS Radio in Atlanta and happened to bump into Commissioner Tagliabue. Innocently, Jack said, "When are you guys going to give St. Louis a franchise?"

As Jack related the story to me the next morning, Tagliabue responded by saying, "Why don't those civic guys get behind Clinton and move this thing forward? It would really enhance their opportunity."

Jack also told me he called Chuck Knight, the head of Emerson Electric, before he had called me but had not reached him, learning that he was in Europe. He left the commissioner's comments with Knight's secretary.

It was after this that I started hearing rumors a new group was being formed with the goal of acquiring the expansion franchise. I was in my office one day when my secretary, Judy Cunetto, walked in and looked as if she had seen a ghost. She had received a telephone call that reminded me of Deep Throat during the Watergate scandal. Judy told me that a man who would not identify himself had just called her on the phone with a very hushed voice and a cryptic message. The caller said he was calling from the office of a downtown firm, where a group of "civic" leaders were having a secret meeting to discuss the pursuit of the expansion team.

Judy told me the caller said, "I admire and respect Mr. Clinton for all he has done. Tell him they are after him, and they are going to get his lease and get the team."

"Who are you? What are you talking about?" Judy responded.

"I can't talk any louder or say anything else," he said. "They are meeting in the next room. Just tell him what I said." Then he hung up.

I also received a phone call from Andy Craig of Boatmen's Bank, who asked me to meet him at the Saint Louis Club. He handed me two copies of a contract, offering to buy out our partnership group for $1 million. I just looked at him.

"Andy, I have well in excess of $5 million in this and you want me to accept this offer and then spread it among Orthwein, Payton, Murray, and myself?" I said. It was an insult.

Some of the pieces were now finally starting to fall into place. I knew there was another group in the shadows working to obtain my share of the lease. I wasn't certain who was involved, but it seemed obvious to me that Andy Craig was involved. I believed this was one of the reasons he had not been more interested in financing my loan request, and perhaps he had gotten to Stan Kroenke before me.

I was really disappointed. I never received a notice that these people were interested in forming a group to try to acquire a football team. Nobody ever invited me to a meeting. I don't know who started the group. Kroenke would have been the perfect lead investor for our group, and I am certain he would have lifted our bid over the top. Instead, his decision to become a part of the new group only made the already muddy waters even murkier.

The confusion reigned for several days, and reports that a second group had been formed began to appear in the media. I was at home watching the 10 p.m. news on KSDK-TV one night, and a report aired that identified several people as being part of the second group. I saw several familiar names and faces.

Craig called me again, this time to tell me how difficult a time he was having trying to get people to pledge money for the project. I could have saved him a lot of time telling him that. He said, "I know what you have been going through."

I found out some members of the new group were people

I had approached and had turned me down. I sat on a bank board with Andy Taylor of Enterprise Leasing, and I never knew he was part of the second group until that night. That really disturbed me. It seemed to me there was a lot of personal motivation in the second group rather than civic interest in trying to do something that was going to make St. Louis a better city.

My feeling was that the NFL leaders wanted me to be involved if they were going to award an expansion franchise to St. Louis. We had built a certain amount of trust in the five years pursuing a team. Those people had gotten to know me personally, and they knew that I had put up the money and had taken all of the risk to build a stadium and get this deal done.

Part of that risk was staging two preseason games to prove that St. Louis would support the NFL. This was an additional expense, since we had to pay the teams coming in for the games—a cost of about $370,000 per team. We also had to have a different structure for ticket prices than you would normally have if you had a "home" team, and of course we had no season-ticket base to rely on. I took a financial bath on those games, but since we filled Busch Stadium we had more ammunition to use in the case we were building for the league.

What the NFL owners could not overlook, however, was the fact that with Kroenke taking the lead investor role in the second group, that group had the one thing I couldn't match— the money necessary to pay the expansion fee. No matter how much the NFL owners liked me personally and wanted me to be involved in the team, they could not give me a team if I didn't have the money. This point was painfully clear to me, and also clear to the second group and the NFL owners.

As the Chicago NFL meeting where the league would be awarding the expansion franchises got closer, it became obvious to me that this second group was trying to use media pressure to force me to pull out of the running and just hand over my lease to them.

Some—not all—members of the media were trying to make me out to be the bad guy, like I was holding onto something I had no business holding onto.

I had paid Fleishman-Hillard more than $1.75 million to prepare public relations materials for the St. Louis NFL partnership.

It didn't help my position when Orthwein came out one day and announced that he would sell his portion of the lease to the new group for one dollar. That again was positioned to make me look like the bad guy. I had invested millions of dollars in this project. Orthwein had already recouped his investment, plus interest. The sale of his portion amounted to a profit for him. A sale of one dollar by me would have been a multimillion-dollar loss.

The media never reported that Orthwein was in a position to sell because he had already been repaid for his investment, plus 5 percent interest, in pursuing a team—by me—and he still was in a very favorable financial position because of his ownership of the Patriots. There was no comparison between his ability to make a grandstand move and look like the good guy riding in on the white horse to save the day and my position. Almost none of the media seemed to understand that.

I was going into the Pasta House headquarters office on the Hill one day for a meeting when I ran into Buzz Westfall. I pulled him aside and said, "Buzz, what is going on?"

He said, "Well, they don't trust Fran Murray."

I couldn't believe this whole nightmare was caused because they didn't trust Fran Murray. I had my doubts about Murray too, but he was not powerful enough to bring this complete deal down, if that was the group's only problem. I told Buzz that Murray could be bought out at a reasonable price rather than an all-or-nothing demand.

Buzz said the group didn't believe it should have to buy out Murray because he hadn't added anything, didn't own anything, and his share wasn't worth anything.

I then asked Buzz what the objections were to me.

"There are two people in the group who don't want any part of you," Buzz told me. When I pressed him, he identified them as Charlie Cella and Sam Fox. I was shocked. "They don't want you to be part of this deal," Buzz said.

I didn't know either Cella or Fox and had no idea why they would object to my involvement in the deal, since I had financed it. Buzz didn't know either, or wouldn't tell me.

We were running out of time; the pressure was mounting. I realized I was facing an impossible task. I knew it was not going to happen.

Al Kerth called me and finally acknowledged the fact that he was working for the second group. He told me that the second group had the financial wherewithal to get the team, and that they would like me to step aside and let them go to Chicago and make the presentation for the good of the city and its football fans.

I told Kerth I thought it would be better if we could meet and put something together so there would be a show of unity when we went to Chicago. Kerth told me that he didn't think that was possible and the second group believed that with the kind of money they were bringing to the table they were confident they could get the team.

Based on my feelings and what I had been told by league officials, I saw it a different way, but it was now out of my control. Kerth asked me to hold a news conference and announce that I was stepping aside in favor of the second group. I told him I would consider doing that. He said he would draft a speech for me for the news conference and send it to me.

Roger Goodell, the NFL executive in charge of expansion, called me again to ask if the second group and I were any closer to reaching an agreement. I told him I had suggested we meet, but the second group said they were not interested.

"Well, I can almost assure you that if they come to Chicago without you they will not get a franchise," he said. I assured

Roger that I had told them that, through Kerth, and he said, "Tell them again." When I told Kerth, he responded, "I have relayed your message to them, and they understand what your message is."

Kerth also had the nerve to ask me to let the second group use the presentation materials which he had prepared—at my expense—and the information Tim Snavely at Peat Marwick had put together—again at my expense—for their presentation. The group never offered to pay me for the materials; they just asked me to turn them over, in the spirit of cooperation. I did so. These were the same people who wanted me to give up my lease for nothing too. I really was amazed by their attitude, but I guess that was the way they were used to conducting their business.

I received the speech from Kerth and scheduled the news conference, but I first had to re-write his speech. His version was a typical PR slant toward the Gateway Partnership, and there was no way I was going to say that. First of all, I had to give credit to my son Jeff, who had closed ranks behind me to run Grey Eagle while I was running around the country trying to get a football team. I told the media and others in the audience that there was no way I would have been able to pursue that effort if I had not had a son ready, willing, and able to run the company behind me. Jeff was there, and I saw him smile. I know he appreciated the comments. Those people just don't think in those terms, so I had to put the comments in my own words.

I also wanted to say a few things about the so-called "civic leaders" of St. Louis, the members of the Civic Progress group; about all of the work that had gone into our effort to bring a football team back to St. Louis and how the so-called "captains of industry" and the banking community had basically turned their backs on me. It was because of this lack of help that I had to step aside and let this mysterious second group go to Chicago to make the presentation. I was talked out of saying this, which was the right thing to do.

However, the city fathers who had formed Civic Progress back in the old days had promoting and improving St. Louis as their number one goal. People like Cubby Bear, Morton May, Edgar Queeny, James McDonnell, John Calhoun, and Gussie Busch were people who really believed in the community and wanted to do whatever they could to make it better. Through the years, most of the new group has evolved from the "captains of industry" to the "soldiers of fortune." I just don't believe the interest is there any more on the corporate level to do things that will make St. Louis a better city. These people seldom reach into their own pocket to do anything for the community. It seems all they do is spend stockholder money. I do believe there are some good people on the Civic Progress board, but unfortunately they have not surfaced as much as I would have liked.

I concluded my news conference by thanking the football fans of St. Louis, and apologizing if I had let them down. The circumstances proved to be that the cost of the team turned out to be far greater than anything we could have anticipated, and we could not generate that sum of money.

It was sad but very gratifying as I drove around to see signs that my retail customers put outside of their businesses thanking me for my efforts. Similar signs showed up on other businesses near the Grey Eagle office. I was reasonably sure the second group was not going to get a team, but of course I could never say that publicly.

Because I had not completed an agreement with the new group regarding the lease, however, I was not going to simply turn it over to them. Kroenke's group went ahead and made its pitch for the expansion team to the NFL owners at the Chicago meeting, but it was no surprise to me when Tagliabue emerged from the meeting and said one of the two expansion franchises had been awarded to Charlotte.

It was a surprise that Tagliabue said the decision on the second city had been delayed until November 30. Clearly, that delay was positioned to give Kroenke's group time to reach an agreement with me regarding the lease, or for me to join their group, and for the league officials to inquire more into the background of Kroenke and the other members of his group.

That night, when Jeff heard the news, he called me all excited. "This is unbelievable," he said. "Maybe you still have a chance for this thing."

I was told that even Chuck Knight said something to the effect that "we're going to have to do a deal with Jerry whether we like it or not." The two people opposing my involvement ultimately won the day.

Again, I was viewed in the major print media as the bad guy. It was incorrectly reported that if I had agreed to give up my lease to the new group, then St. Louis would have been awarded the team. There was no way that was going to happen at that meeting. As deliberate and thorough as the NFL is, there was no way they were going to vote to give a team to somebody they didn't even know had existed until a month earlier. I had written a letter to Tagliabue and told him the lease would not be a problem. If St. Louis was awarded a team, we would be able to come to an agreement on the lease.

Another misconception by a lot of people was that the lease was the only reason Kroenke's group was denied the team at that time. The NFL, behind closed doors, had to be confident that if it awarded the franchise to St. Louis I would be forced to cut a deal with the group concerning the lease. Kroenke's group had even told the league they were prepared to play for two seasons in Busch Stadium, until my hold on the lease expired. Then they would negotiate a lease and move into the dome.

I don't think the league cared about that. If St. Louis had been awarded the team there would have been no way I could have held onto the lease. I couldn't block the team from coming here! There was no way I could have held onto the lease unless I wanted to move to the moon. The league knew that, and Kroenke's group knew that.

Running a company such as Grey Eagle, which requires the public to buy your product to be successful, would have forced my hand. It would have been a marketing disaster to try to run Grey Eagle while keeping an NFL team from moving to St. Louis. There was no way Anheuser-Busch would have let that happen.

I think the NFL truly thought that delaying the second city selection for a month would give us time to come to an agreement, but it didn't happen. When it came down to a final decision, the NFL was reluctant to force the issue since we couldn't voluntarily come together. It was a much simpler decision to award the second franchise to Jacksonville.

The expansion and finance committees recommended Jacksonville by a 10–2 vote. The two negative votes were cast by owners who wanted the team to go to Baltimore. Then came the vote by the full ownership, and this time it was 26–2 in favor of Jacksonville. The only negative votes came from Norman Braman of Philadelphia and Orthwein.

That night I was the guest at a reunion of former boxers at the South Broadway Athletic Club. While the news of the day had not been a surprise, it still marked a major disappointment. I have never been an easy loser.

Suddenly a "runner" from KMOV-TV came up to me and said his station wanted me to return to Channel 4, as the second group had returned from Chicago and was holding a press conference at the airport, blaming me for them being turned down a second time. Knight and Cella were still calling for me to "give" them the lease. The electronic press was very kind to me after reviewing the embarrassing "press conference." They gave me a chance to respond to their ranting and raving! It was not our city's finest hour.

The best chance for St. Louis to get an expansion team would have been for the two groups to merge forces. It would have been very easy and simple to do, and everyone would have been happy. I never said I had to be in control. I would have been very satisfied with a small percentage of the team. It never came close to happening.

What bothered me most in the weeks and months that followed was all of the finger-pointing and the print media playing the blame game, wondering what had gone wrong and where to cast the blame. I never liked that game, and I hated it even more then.

And while the expansion game might have ended, another game was just beginning.

My sons Jeff and Brian help me welcome our employees and guests to Grey Eagle's annual celebration at Eagle Estate.

In the center of the picture, you will see prominent attorney Scott Rosenblum, who married Grey Eagle secretary Georgeanne, who is at his side.

A view toward the lake at Eagle Estate.

The Grey Eagle management team at Puerto Vallarta, Mexico, between budget meetings. Left standing: Don Sorich, me, Buz Schoo. Front row: Jeff Clinton, Jenny Boone, Judy Cunetto, Neil Komadoski, Steve Nolan, and Steve Jones.

Doc Severinsen and the NBC Orchestra at the Grey Eagle 25th Anniversary.

This photo is from a cocktail party at the Log Cabin Club hosted by Robert F. Hyland (left), CBS vice president and general manager of KMOX Radio. Mr. Hyland didn't think I had received enough recognition for my effort to bring the NFL to St. Louis. Therefore, he felt a need to carry the message. He was a great gentleman.

My last picnic, "A Fair to Remember," featured a fifty-foot Ferris Wheel.

Lee Roarty and Carole Buck ride with Carole and Jack's grandson. (He looks like Jack, doesn't he?!)

The Pasta House's Kim Tucci and his wife Sharon take their turn.

Julie Buck and another of her sons share a ride.

My guys! Front row: Riley, Mark, and Nathan. In grandpa's arms: Myles and Cole.

This was the last portrait Jeff had made with his sons, Mark and Nate, December 2001. They were very special to him.

The Mizzou Arena Club was named in memory of Jeff. Here, Mike Alden helps Jim Koman and me cut the ribbon.

I was always so proud to share our employee picnics with my son Jeff.

Jim Koman and I at the Mizzou Arena Club dedication. The inside bar carrying Jeff's name (in background) is prominent under the Missouri "M."

Always a large number of sports figures attend the annual Budweiser Guns and Hoses!

Col. Jerry Lee, Terri Larkin, me, and Col. Ron Battelle at a Rams game.

John Forsyth, Robin Smith, and Carol Lawrence join me at the Variety Club's Dinner with the Stars, c. 1989.

Fran Murray, me, and Walter Payton being proclamated by the mayor's office for our work to return the NFL to St. Louis.

Buzz Westfall, Pat Hannon, and Ramon Gallardo enjoy the festivities at an annual Grey Eagle celebration at Eagle Estate.

Anheuser-Busch's Tony Ponturo and Mike Roarty, along with KMOV-TV General Manager Alan Cohen, present me with the Variety Champion for Children's Award for 2003.

Pals Stan Musial, Mike Roarty, and Jack Buck join me ringside for a Budweiser Guns and Hoses Tournament.

Mayor Francis Slay and Alderwoman Phyllis Young present me with the sign that will be hung on Convention Plaza Dr., which by Aldermanic Law will be forever known as "Jerry Clinton Way" in honor of my work to pass legislation to build the domed stadium.

I'm being honored by my son Jeff and dear friend Jack Buck for my charity work. This photo is very special to me. I miss them very much!

My former partner, Bob McNamara, and me pushing "the product," c. 1975.

Terri Larkin and I are out with our great friend Marshall Faulk.

August A. Busch IV and me on the night before August and Kate were married.

My old pal Ed McMahon and I enjoy after-dinner cigars while vacationing in St. Martin, FWI.

Chapter *11*

ONE OF THE REASONS WE had insisted on holding onto the lease for the stadium for two years following the selection of the expansion teams was because we knew there was no guarantee that we would be awarded one of those teams. We also knew that, following the expansion selections, there would be teams looking to relocate. We wanted to be in a position to lure one of those teams to St. Louis, and we thought we were.

Instead of looking forward, which I wanted to do, much of the St. Louis media wanted to look back—and continue to examine why St. Louis had been passed over in favor of Charlotte and Jacksonville as expansion cities.

As our group began to talk to other teams about the potential for moving an existing NFL team to St. Louis, several media members in town continued to criticize me and say my refusal to "give up" the lease to Kroenke's group had been the principle reason St. Louis did not receive a team.

Now, "they" were saying St. Louis was going to have the same problem in our next attempt to land a team.

My biggest critics in the media were Bernie Miklasz and Jim Thomas of the *Post-Dispatch* and Mike Bush of KSDK-TV, the sports director of the St. Louis NBC affiliate. Other people in the media were much more understanding of my situation, such as Jack Buck, Ron Jacober, Mark Curtis, Kevin Slaten, and Mike Claiborne, to name just a few.

At one time I thought I had a good, or at least a professional, relationship with Miklasz, Thomas, and Bush, but somewhere along the line that changed. I had a basic philosophical difference with the *Post-Dispatch* as well. A few years earlier, I had loaned my motor coach to Jack Buck and his family when he was inducted into the Baseball Hall of Fame in Cooperstown, N.Y., and later I did the same thing when both Dan Dierdorf and Jackie Smith were inducted into the Pro Football Hall of Fame in Canton, Ohio.

We loaded the coach with beer for their tailgate parties and personal entertaining. Two *Post-Dispatch* employees who covered Jackie's induction came to the after-party and mingled with the crowd and wrote stories about it. Miklasz and Thomas never mentioned how I had provided Jackie with the motor coach. In an effort to try to understand their attitude, I arranged a meeting with one of the newspaper's editors at the Missouri Athletic Club.

When I showed up at the meeting with my lawyer, Jim Shoemake, the editor started to get up to leave. Finally, I convinced him to stay and told him about what had happened.

"You mean to tell me that you were there and they didn't write it in the paper?" the editor said. "That's exactly what I'm telling you." I said. "Well that's derelict in their duty as journalists," he said.

I thought he was sincere and that something might come out of it, but it was not too long after our discussion when the editor left the paper and moved from St. Louis. Nothing ever came out of that meeting that I know of.

Miklasz at one time had been in my corner. In September 1993, after I bought out Orthwein and took full control of our partnership, he wrote a column headlined "Clinton deserves to call signals." In the column he said, "It is my opinion, hope you agree, that Clinton will be an ideal owner of a St. Louis football franchise."

It is not unusual that public relations professionals feed information to media outlets to suit their own purposes. I believe that happened in this case. Stories in the print media were definitely slanted. I thought, "What a shame as a professional journalist to be used for the private interest of others."

At one point I had a good relationship with Thomas, the football beat writer for the *Post*. He came to the Road America racetrack in Wisconsin to write a story about me and Walter Payton when we were driving race cars, and Jim and I always had cordial, respectful conversations while the expansion effort was progressing.

That all changed when he came to my office for an interview when we were in the midst of trying to put our investor group together before going to the expansion meeting in Chicago. Thomas asked me questions that I really wasn't in a position to answer, and he became very belligerent when I kept repeating that I wasn't going to say anything more than "no comment." He wanted to know who our lead investor was going to be, and I had promised to keep that information secret. Thomas kept insisting that I tell him who it was.

After a few minutes Thomas got up from his chair and raised his voice at me. I was stunned. He had never acted like that before. I sat and stared at him, too surprised to react immediately. Finally, I stood up and came out from behind my desk and said, "This interview is over. Get out of my office."

From that point on our relationship changed, so much so that by the time our group had begun discussions with John Shaw, the president of the Los Angeles Rams, about the possibility of moving the team from Anaheim to St. Louis, Thomas wrote a story in the newspaper with the headline, "Clinton becoming an obstructionist." The story went on to say, "Clinton's sole interest isn't securing a football team for St. Louis. It's securing a football team for St. Louis that he can be a part of."

The ink on the paper was probably still wet when my phone rang at home that morning. It was Jack Buck calling, asking if I had read the newspaper. I replied that yes, I had seen it.

Jack was furious. He said, "I want you to come on my radio show tonight on KMOX, and then I want Thomas on to explain why he feels he needed to attack you. Then, if needed, you can come back on and make your points and have the last say in rebuttal, if needed. I can't stand it I'm so mad."

Of course I agreed to go on, and made my comments, but unfortunately I don't think as many people heard that radio show as probably read the story in the newspaper that morning. It just seemed, for whatever reason, from that point on there was a little collusion going on between Miklasz and Thomas. They seemed to always be on the same subject at the same time. If something changed a little bit, they both changed at the same time.

Two days after Thomas' "obstructionist" story appeared, Miklasz wrote a column headlined "Jerry, it's not personal, we just disagree." Included in the column was this comment, "Clinton feels betrayed. He's been going on radio and TV this week, accusing the *Post-Dispatch* of being 'out to get' him.

"Why, because certain views conflict with his? Everyone has a right to an opinion. We have a right to disagree with each other. Sports columnists have a right to adjust as volatile news stories evolve."

A month later, as negotiations with the Rams were at a critical stage, Miklasz was back at it again. "Memo to Rams, Clinton doesn't speak for city." The lead to his column said, "By now the most intelligent thing to do is ignore Jerry Clinton. Like a petulant child who has been sent to the corner and denied a coveted toy, he wails with the desperate hope that someone will take pity. I regret that I am accommodating his desire for attention." It seems Bernie is guilty of those things he accuses of me.

How could anybody think that was anything other than a personal attack? Miklasz had not been present when Shoemake and I met with John Shaw. He had not been on the extension in the bedroom when Shaw and I talked on the telephone. He was not privy to those discussions; he never got a copy of the communications that were sent back and forth. I personally believe this was his way of trying to force this information from me, but as Buzz Westfall found, you can't negotiate these deals in the media. Buzz and Freeman Bosley Jr., who had followed Schoemehl as St. Louis' mayor, had formed another group, called FANS Inc., in order to represent the interests of the city and county in the pursuit of a team. Buzz spoke to the media after returning from the first FANS Inc. meeting in Los Angeles. When Shaw read his comments, he announced there would be no more meetings. Former U.S. Senator Tom Eagleton was then brought in as the spokesman for the group.

Miklasz and Thomas both thought they knew everything that was going on, but they were wrong. They also were wrong in thinking that everybody cared what they thought. They have no accountability and it seems no responsibility. They can write whatever they want on a daily basis and nobody responds to those attacks.

One of the things I didn't understand was how I could have the support of most of the influential labor unions in the community and from the public but could not get better treatment by some of the media. I have letters of support—which actually were resolutions—from Robert J. Kelley, President of the Greater St. Louis Labor Council; and from my childhood friend Bob Sansone, then the Executive-Secretary Treasurer of the Building and Construction Trades Council of St. Louis, AFL-CIO. I certainly appreciated their support and all of the support of the union members, which I knew meant that not everybody in St. Louis believed what Miklasz and Thomas were writing in the newspaper.

Personally, I could have cared less what they or anybody else in the media said about me. What hurt me the most, however, was that my father, Harry, had to read these columns in the newspaper about his son. He didn't know everything that was going on, and in addition, he was quite ill. It hurt him deeply that these reporters were attacking and criticizing his son.

He called me on the phone and said. "Why are these people writing these stories about you?" I had to tell him it was simply their opinions and that it was not the majority opinion around the city. He felt bad because he thought it was making his son look bad in the community.

My father was watching the news one night when Mike Bush came out and said, "Jerry Clinton is a bad guy." He called me and said, "Why would he say something like that?"

Part of the media's problem is that they really think they are more important than they are, but they also don't take time to realize the impact of what they say and what they report. Have you ever noticed that an accusation can be in large, bold headlines on the front page of the newspaper but the corrections and retractions are printed in small, regular type on page 18-C? The paper doesn't want its readers to know they were wrong.

Many media people want to make themselves the story, and that causes even more problems. I didn't care what Thomas and Miklasz wrote about me, because I knew the truth. I also didn't think John Shaw and the Rams were going to be influenced by the media. However, I do believe they hurt St. Louis with the league.

A decade later, respected St. Louis senior television news anchor Dick Ford said at his retirement party, "As reporters of the news you should never try to make yourself look good while making others look bad." Ethical news reporting has deteriorated over the years, and that's a shame. The reporters who believed in a higher ethical standard like Buck, Ford, and others I have mentioned carry and deserve a higher degree of respect from the community.

When Shoemake and I met with Shaw at an NFL owners meeting in Coral Gables, Florida, in May 1994, he gave us a list of six conditions that the Rams were looking to meet from any city they would consider moving to. Shoemake wrote them down longhand on a sheet of yellow legal paper. None of them was considered a major obstacle.

Shaw said that if we could satisfy the Rams' concerns on those six issues, then he thought we could reach an agreement. We went back to St. Louis and prepared our response on the issues, and I was encouraged that our talks were going to continue.

While we initiated discussions with the Rams, FANS Inc. stepped in front of us, and during this time Shoemake received a call from an acquaintance of his who happened to be on the board of trustees of the Tampa Bay Buccaneers.

The owner of the team, Hugh Culverhouse Sr., died in August 1994, and his son, Hugh Jr., had decided he did not want to take over the team and would like to see it sold. Hugh Jr. and I had met a few times during the league meetings, enjoying a couple of cold Budweisers on occasion, and he told the board that if everything could be worked out he would like to see me get the team. Shoemake, two of our potential investors, and I flew to Tampa and had a very good meeting with the board. We wanted to keep our options open, knowing we still could not be certain how the talks with Shaw and the Rams would turn out.

The board had set the price of the Buccaneers at $187 million and asked our group if that price was acceptable. The new potential lead investor produced documentation from Bear Sterns in New York that the money was available. We agreed that it was and said that we had the money.

The biggest obstacle to overcome was an NFL requirement that required a team with the desire to relocate to file a three-year plan with the league stating that there was a desire to move the team. Without that notice, the league would not approve a move.

Our option was to buy the team, put that plan in place, and operate the team in Tampa for three years before moving it St. Louis. This option would not have worked for several reasons. One, the Tampa franchise was already in serious financial trouble, and if we came in and announced we would be moving the team to St. Louis in three years, then nobody would have come to the games and the interest in the team would have totally collapsed.

Secondly, we only controlled the lease at the dome in St. Louis for two years. If we had to wait for three years before we could move the team, we would have had to negotiate a new stadium lease in St. Louis.

We were hung up on that problem during the meeting when I suggested we take a break. When we returned to the table, one of the trustees said he thought he had a solution. He suggested we put the $187 million in an escrow account, then they would move the team to St. Louis. Once the league had signed off on the move, then we could take over the team and they would take over the escrow account. Culverhouse, who had owned the Bucs since they came into the league in 1976, thought that if they were the ones moving the team, then they could get around the three-year plan requirement.

The problem with this plan, even if it had been approved by the league, was that the trustees wanted us to put up a $10 million non-refundable deposit. They said that money would be forfeited if for any reason the deal did not get done. Our group, and the lead investor, would not agree to that. We had already invested too much money and again, with no guarantees, there was no way we could take on that additional financial risk.

Part of our concern was that we knew FANS Inc. was also talking to John Shaw and the Rams. By that time Eagleton had taken over for Westfall in negotiating for the group, and we called Eagleton and asked if he could hold off on those discussions for a brief time to give our group a chance to try to finalize the deal with Tampa Bay. Eagleton's response was, "My bosses won't let me."

I said, "Who are your bosses?" He said, "I can't tell you, but their initials are CP." CP of course meant Civic Progress to me. I don't know if things could have been different if Westfall had not been replaced by Eagleton, but Buzz had backed off when he thought his involvement might have ramifications on his position as St. Louis County Executive. He told me he still had to be re-elected twice to guarantee his retirement.

The FANS Inc. group then turned to Eagleton, who had been accustomed to giving away other people's money for years. He was very good at it and does it with great flare. I was concerned again, because this looked as if it was going to be the expansion process all over again. If these discussions boiled down solely to money, FANS Inc. still represented a much wealthier group of St. Louis than we did, and suddenly I was going to be the low man on the totem pole again.

When we knew we could not get the deal done in Tampa, and it looked certain that the FANS Inc. group was going to be able to give Shaw, the Rams, and owner Georgia Frontiere a much more lucrative deal than we could give them, I knew the only matter left to address was to negotiate the sale of my 30 percent share of the lease.

I have never and will never criticize John Shaw and the Rams for agreeing to the deal with FANS Inc. I applauded him for it. I would have done the same thing in his position. Ultimately and primarily, St. Louis paid for everything, through the sale of PSLs, personal seat licenses.

When I realized the lease was going to be surrendered, my concern shifted to being able to recoup the costs I had incurred trying to bring a football stadium and a team to St. Louis. Two national accounting firms independently reached the same figure—$8 million. It really was more than that if you took into account the sweat equity, or the use of my plane to attend different meetings, and the work people at my company did that I never charged to the partnership, but the figure of $8 million was acceptable to me.

The FANS Inc. lawyers tried to get me to accept a deal between $4 million and $5 million, but I said no. I didn't think I had to take a personal loss for my contribution to build a domed stadium and position St. Louis as a worthy city to become the home of a National Football League team. I wanted to be reimbursed for everything I had spent, and I would not accept one penny less. They finally agreed. I had one additional stipulation—that no local ownership group could own the lease; it had to go to an existing NFL team.

As I told the owners group in Chicago during the expansion process, it was never my intention or desire to own an NFL franchise. My desire was to help the City of St. Louis retain its first-class status, and to do that I thought we needed an NFL team and a domed stadium, which is used now for so much more than ten football games a year. I was very satisfied when I signed the deal to turn over the lease. My goals had been met—St. Louis was getting back into the NFL and my efforts had been repaid. I wanted it to be a fair deal, and I wanted to be treated fairly. Plenty of people were involved in this process, however, who I felt didn't understand what that meant.

There is no place in the dome where you will see or read the name Jerry Clinton. There is a small sign outside the dome that proclaims a short section of the street as "Jerry Clinton Way." I am not saying I want more recognition than that, but I do want people to know the truth. And that is, there can be a strange elitist undertow in our beloved community.

When the NFL officially approved the transfer of the Rams to St. Louis, Miklasz took another indirect shot at me in his column. He said, "No city has invested more time, money, effort or emotion into the procurement of a National Football League franchise. This experience was a long, primal scream. And we won. We did it. Really. We beat the tough guys."

Bernie, I don't know how you could include yourself in the "we" category, since you had more to do with creating a negative atmosphere for the project than most anyone.

One of the problems with having only one newspaper in a city is that people often take what is reported on those pages as the truth, when sometimes it could not be more wrong. I had that conversation a few years later with Terry Egger when he was the publisher of the *Post-Dispatch*.

I happened to run into Terry at a Christmas party of the 1-2-3 Club, a group of sports and media people in St. Louis, and mentioned to him how unfairly critical I thought the *Post's* coverage of me had been over the years. "Why can't we set the record straight?" I said. "I'm concerned because your people wrote bad and untrue things about me and that's now a piece of the public record. They criticized me and called me names like 'the street fighter' and 'obstructionist' and things like that." He said, "Maybe we'll have a chance to do that."

"I'm only concerned because of the public record aspects of it," I said. "When I die, what are they going to print from the archives? I'm afraid it will be negative stuff, and I don't think my family deserves that."

Terry said the newspaper would be doing a story on the 10th anniversary of the Rams moving to St. Louis and that maybe it would be the opportunity for me to finally speak my peace. I said I would appreciate that, and we both went on our way.

A few months later, a young female reporter called and said she was assigned to interview me about my role in building the stadium and the effort to bring football back to St. Louis. I thought this was finally going to be a chance for the *Post-Dispatch* to give credit where credit was due, and set the record straight. This reporter wasn't in St. Louis during that period of time and therefore had not been influenced by others at the *Post-Dispatch*.

I was wrong again. When the story was published, it included the line, "He thought he should be rewarded not only for his hard work, but for the money he invested."

Rewarded? What kind of nonsense was that? I was incensed. The word "reward" had never been used during the interview. I knew that because I had tape-recorded the interview.

I telephoned the reporter and said I really objected to the use of the word "rewarded" in the story. She should have used my word, "reimbursed," which was exactly the truth and the word I had used. But it was changed to "rewarded." What was the reason for the change?

She had an original comeback: "I didn't do it."

"Well who did?" I asked.

It must have been one of her editors, she said. I asked if she knew the difference between reimburse and reward. She said yes, but the editor must have changed it for some reason.

"I want a retraction," I said. "Normally I wouldn't ask for that but this is a matter of public record. I asked that my story be printed as I knew it, and this is certainly not in keeping with Terry Egger's promise to me." She said she would call me back.

She did call back the next day and said she had talked with her editors about the situation and that they did not think it was important enough to print a retraction. "That makes the situation even less credible for the *Post-Dispatch*," I said. They deliberately changed the story to suit their own purposes. It was not part of the interview, and changing that one word changed the whole complexion of the story as far as I was concerned.

That is the type of newspaper we have in St. Louis. I know that if the paper slanted the story on this occasion then there had to be other times the "editors" have tweaked a story to make it a little more exciting or compelling or whatever they want it to be. They think it might help them sell a few more newspapers, but I think it just shows ethics are not alive and well at the *Post-Dispatch* in my opinion.

I ran into Terry at another luncheon a few weeks later and told him he was not going to believe what happened. He apologized and said he was sorry. I said, "I am too Terry."

I was tired of being so squarely in the public eye. I was glad when the Rams came to St. Louis, and my involvement with the NFL ended, except for going to the games and cheering the team on like the rest of the fans.

I was ready to get on with the rest of my life.

Chapter *12*

I HAD BEEN SO IMMERSED in the pursuit of a football team—devoting most of my life to the project for seven years—that I knew it was going to take some time to figure out what I wanted to do next, to see what challenge would present itself.

One thing I knew was that I was going to continue to be involved with, and support, charitable efforts in the St. Louis community, primarily for the Backstoppers and children's charities.

When I had become involved with Grey Eagle, I realized very quickly that we had been presented with a community responsibility. We had a license to sell alcohol beverages, but along with that license came that responsibility. It was incumbent on us to craft our business activities, and to use our business to become as much of a positive influence on the community as possible.

Obviously our goal was to sell as much beer and other beverages as possible. Along with meeting that goal, however, was the realization that we had to develop programs that would educate the consumers about the dangers of drinking and driving. We were the first wholesaler, and maybe the first company in the country, to develop an anti-drinking and driving program in 1982, called None for the Road. I'm glad to say many other programs have been developed over the years, and the result has been a decline in both deaths caused by accidents related to drinking and deaths of minors that could be attributed to drinking.

Grey Eagle, along with Anheuser-Busch, helped develop the Alert Cab program in the St. Louis community. The program provides consumers who have had too much to drink in a public place with a free cab ride home and a free ride back the next day to pick up their car. The cost is paid for by Grey Eagle, Lohr Distributors, Anheuser-Busch, and the cab company. These programs are examples of ways that we can help ourselves be responsible.

I learned early on that if we didn't help ourselves by coming up with these programs, the legislators would provide help for us, which wouldn't necessarily be the kind of help that is conducive to a healthy business environment.

There is an obvious connection between beer and sports, and being a sports-minded individual, I looked for opportunities where we could sell and market our product through sporting and recreational events. I also looked for opportunities where we could give something back to the community, and that was how we came up with the Guns and Hoses boxing event between police officers and firefighters.

In the mid-1980s, Jerry Lisker of New York and I had struck up a friendship with Butch Lewis, the boxing promoter. Jerry worked for Rupert Murdoch in New York and had been a Golden Glove boxer as a kid, just like me. He knew I had supported the Golden Gloves for years and had staged a boxing card on the *Admiral* riverboat.

We got together occasionally, and one time Jerry came to St. Louis with a couple of New York police officers assigned to the police pension fund, working to raise money for the charity. Jerry suggested that we put together a team of boxers from the St. Louis police department and come to New York to fight a team of New York officers. We would then split the proceeds among our various charities.

Jerry said they had a similar event in which the New York officers fought the London Bobbies, and it had been very successful.

I told Jerry I would think about it and get back to him in a few days. I called Myrl Taylor, the head of the St. Louis chapter of USA boxing, and asked him what he thought of the idea.

"It's a little scary to me," Myrl said. "The police officers I have seen are in their forties and fifties and probably average about forty pounds overweight. I think the New York officers involved are probably more experienced and active boxers."

I agreed with Myrl and then said, "Well if it works in New York, why don't we get our own police officers to compete against our firefighters and see where that takes us." Myrl agreed, and the Budweiser Boxing Showdown was born.

We staged the first event in 1987, and it quickly caught on. We expanded the fight card to include other jurisdictions besides the city and St. Louis County and now have teams of firefighters boxing against the police officers. That's when we were able to change the title name from Showdown to Budweiser Guns and Hoses. We even have female bouts, which have proved to be very popular. We never found a need to go to New York.

My nephew Kevin Clinton fought four times, twice as a city police officer and twice as a county officer, and has four trophies at home to show for his four victories.

The event benefits Backstoppers, the organization that supports the families of police officers and firefighters killed in the line of duty. The organization comes forward following the death of the officer or firefighter and provides emergency cash to get through the early days, then comes back and sets up programs to pay the home mortgage and the educational expenses of the victim's children. It is a wonderful organization and provides a great service to our community.

The 9-11 tragedy in 2001 brought increased awareness and drove home the point that the police officers and firefighters are the true heroes of our community. They are the first responders to any alarm, and they constantly put their lives on the line to keep our lives and property safe. I like to be involved with win-win situations, and they don't come any better than this one.

Over the eighteen years we have staged Guns and Hoses— now always the night before Thanksgiving at the Savvis Center— we have raised more than $1.6 million for Backstoppers.

Some of the individuals who were involved as competitors in the early days are now working as coaches for some of the boxers, and it has been extremely rewarding to see what this event means to them and how it has continued to grow. I think it is an event that will continue for years to come, even though we hope there is never a need for additional funds . . . reality tells us that need will come.

Another charity in which I became actively involved and supported was Marygrove, a center for abused children who need a safe place to live with counseling and help. Florissant Mayor Jim Eagen called my office one day and asked me to visit Marygrove with him, and when I did I instantly knew it was a cause I had to support. I became a board member, and over the years Jeff also got involved, even himself becoming a member of the Marygrove board of directors.

Marygrove has helped so many kids over the years because it provides them with a safe and comfortable environment where they can go and get the help they need while they are restoring their lives.

I gave a speech one time in which I talked about why I was so interested in children's charities. The principle reason, I said, was because the children did not choose to put themselves in bad situations. Children don't choose to be born as crack babies or with tuberculosis or cystic fibrosis. Children don't choose to be born into severe poverty or without limbs or organs. These are not their choices, which is why those children need our help.

You have to give them a fighting chance to improve their lives and to become citizens who will have a good quality of life and be able to function as useful and productive members of society. When adults get into trouble, often times it is as a result of a bad choice that they made. They had a choice and chose the wrong direction. Nobody ever gave these children that choice.

I have also been involved with Variety Kids, a charity that supports children, usually with mental and physical handicaps. For the past five years, I have financially supported the Children's

Chorus. I have also helped raise more than $1 million for cancer causes, including helping to provide mammograms for women who otherwise could not afford them. I regularly donate to Kids in the Middle, a counseling program for children whose parents are going through a divorce and separations. Now I have the privilege of serving on the board of the Asthma and Allergy Foundation, which helps raise money to get the necessary medicine for children who cannot afford it. Kids with asthma miss an average of fifty days of school a year, usually because they do not have the proper medication.

I enjoy being involved with these organizations, and I have been fortunate to be in a business that has provided me the opportunity to help support these causes financially and by serving on various boards of directors. It has been extremely rewarding.

As Jeff was taking on more of a leadership role at Grey Eagle, I really believed that these charities held my future. I would have the time to work for the best interests of these charities while pursuing my personal interests, including boating and golf.

One terrible, horrible morning, those hopes and plans changed.

Chapter *13*

ONE FACET OF MY LIFE that I certainly was most proud of was how well my two sons, Jeff and Brian, had grown into outstanding young men. Their mother, Jo, did an outstanding job of raising them when I was busy working. They were both great kids who enjoyed all of the normal childhood activities.

I had fun coaching their Little League baseball and soccer teams, although Jeff had to endure many more years of my coaching than Brian did.

One thing I learned early on about Jeff's personality was how fierce a competitor he was. It didn't matter what the activity was—if there was a winner and a loser, Jeff's goal was to be the winner. If his team would lose a game he would come straight home and go into his room and sit there and sulk. He had to think about what had happened in the game before he would come out and rejoin the family.

It always bothered me, and I tried to keep him from doing that. I tried to explain to him about team competition and how your team was not always going to win, but I don't know whether he ever really agreed with me. Losing was always for the other guy.

Jeff went to Chaminade High School and played baseball and a little football. Brian went to CBC and played football and was on the swim team. Brian played sports for the sake of participation; Jeff was always a lot more serious about it. Everything was always about winning and losing with Jeff.

Over the years Jeff and I had our share of disagreements, and his mother always said it was because we were so much alike. We were both stubborn in our ways and driven, to a certain extent.

Jeff and Brian were far enough apart in age—five years—that they didn't really play together as much as did brothers who were closer in age. Jeff always had energy to burn. He would wake up on a Saturday morning and grab the family lawnmower and head down the street to mow lawns to make some money. Brian was very content to wake up and spend the morning on the couch watching cartoons.

Jeff was obviously a Type A personality, and Brian was more laid back. Those personalities stuck with them over the years, and I don't think I was ever more surprised than when Jeff and I both started racing cars, Brian came up and said he wanted to race too.

He went to the racing school, and the first time I saw him race I was totally amazed at how aggressive he was. He had great ability driving a racecar. Jeff used to stand there watching him and laugh and say, "Dad, he's better than both of us." He would keep the accelerator on the floor all the way down the straightaway into the corners. He won several races and was Rookie of the Year in the region, the same award Jeff and I also won.

Brian lost interest in racing over the years and developed other interests. We really had fun when all of us were involved, making it a social event by taking the motor coach to the track and having cookouts and inviting all of our friends to come by.

I was always more nervous watching Jeff and Brian race than when I was in the car myself. I think all racers are like that; you never think anything is going to happen to you. There is always an element of danger involved in the sport, but it is just so exhilarating that when you are in the car you tend to forget about it. When you finish a race, whether you won or lost, as long as you did your best, there was a great feeling of accomplishment.

It really surprised me that both Jeff and Brian said they wanted to race. Jeff was older and had really objected when I started racing. He was so opposed to my driving that I never thought he would want to participate as a competitor. However, he showed a great talent for success.

He took his time advancing to higher horsepower cars, but he always knew his limitations. He was very cautious about overestimating his abilities. I remember testing my 550 horsepower car at the Gateway International track and asked him if he wanted to take it out for a few laps. He gave me a shy grin and said, "No Dad, I'm not ready for that yet." He was very careful about not moving up too quickly.

Jeff was much more of an accomplished driver than I was. He won two national championships and was moving into the professional ranks. He developed a team with two other drivers to race a prototype car in the NASPORT series, a division of NASCAR owned by Bill France. It was an open cockpit car with a roll bar across the top.

We spoke about my wish that he race more GT types of cars, which offered a lot more protection because you had a roof and were basically sitting inside a roll cage. The open cockpit cars always worried me because of the exposure of the head and upper body if something did go wrong, especially from a frontal impact. I told him with his position with Grey Eagle and as the father of two young boys that I felt he should be competing in a car which offered more protection. I told him that to enjoy racing he didn't have to drive that type of car. He was confident in the car and tried to reassure me that the car was safe. He said he wanted to race for one more year and then would do something different.

I never went to any of those races. Jeff was always serious about racing, but I didn't feel some of the people that he was involved with were as serious as Jeff. They seemed to have a lot of play in them. I know he was talked into it by his teammates because he brought the Budweiser label to the racing team.

I tried to block out thoughts about Jeff racing that car as much as possible. On March 1, 2002, I knew he was at Homestead, Florida, practicing for an upcoming race. I had gone out to my country place because I was meeting with a builder and an architect.

It was about 11:30 in the morning when I received a call on my cell phone. It was Steve Nolan, then a vice president of Grey Eagle. He said, "Jerry, I have some very bad news." I said, "What is it Steve?"

There was silence on the other end of the phone. "Steve, is it Jeff?" I said. "Yes, he was in a bad crash," Steve said.

"Steve, is he dead?" I said. Steve paused for a moment and then said, "Yes."

I just remember becoming totally numb. My first thought was, "My God, how am I going to tell his mother?" She was at her home in Sanibel, Florida, where she lived by herself. I knew I was in shock, and I had a million thoughts running through my mind.

I told Rosie, who manages my country property, that I had to leave. She had heard me on the phone and knew what had happened. I got in the car and headed back toward St. Louis, driving east on I-70. I don't remember driving. I do remember pulling over to the side of the road when it hit me that "My God, nobody has told Brian."

I called Brian and told him his brother had been killed. Jeff was thirty-eight years old. It just seemed so unfair.

Brian was in shock too, but he has always been very levelheaded. I told him I had to call their mother. He had the phone numbers for two of her best friends who lived near her, and I asked him to call them and see if they could go over to her house to be with her when I told her what had happened. I told Brian to give them my cell phone number and for them to call me when they got to the house.

When I got the call that they were there, I made the call to break the horrible news to Jo. She was devastated. She handed the phone to one of her friends and I asked the friend to call her doctor and get him to prescribe a sedative. I said I would be coming down on the plane later that afternoon to pick her up and bring her back to St. Louis.

I still really didn't know any details of what had happened. There would be time to figure that out.

Brian and his wife Megan met me and went with me on the plane to Florida to pick up Jo. She had always enjoyed watching him race simply because he was so darn good at it. We all were still in shock, just going through the motions, doing what we knew we needed to do. I'm not sure how we did it.

It was the worst day of my life.

During my flight to Florida and the return flight to St. Louis, I was not aware of the great outpouring of shock and sympathy for my family. People were calling in to radio stations to express their feelings. My office received more than 200 phone calls. The volume was so heavy that my secretary, Judy, needed help from my friend Mike Drohlich, a public relations executive, to answer all the calls.

It was obvious to those near me that the shock of this event had penetrated deeply into our community. A bright light had been violently snuffed out. I knew the days and weeks ahead would be dark and difficult.

The source of much pain was not only that Jo and I had lost a beloved son and Brian a brother, but two little boys, Mark, 5, and Nathan, 3, had lost their Daddy with whom they did so many fun things and loved so much.

A million thoughts were all colliding in my head at once during those first few days after Jeff's death. There was a delay in releasing his body from the Dade County coroner's office, so we could not schedule the funeral until five days later, on March 6.

The dark days were filled with family and friends converging on my house, and we reached out to each other to get through the ordeal. Sitting in the funeral parlor, making the arrangements, it all seemed surreal. "This doesn't seem like it could possibly be true . . . what are we doing here, what is this all about." I know everybody who has lost a family member to a sudden and tragic death has exactly those same thoughts.

With the huge outpouring of sympathy, both locally and nationally, I realized our local Ste. Genevieve du Bois parish was not going to be large enough to accommodate everybody who wanted to attend the funeral mass. At the suggestion of Father John Schemlefler, I called the archdiocese office, and after receiving their condolences I was told, "On Wednesday the Basilica belongs to your son."

On the day of the wake, I received a phone call from August Busch III, who was in New Orleans, where Anheuser-Busch was holding their national sales conference. He wanted to know what time I would be at the funeral home, and I told him the visitation started at 2 p.m. He and several other Anheuser-Busch executives left the sales conference and flew back to St. Louis, and they were in line promptly at 2 p.m. I really appreciated his thoughtfulness and friendship.

The line of mourners ran outside the funeral home onto the street. It was continuous from 2 p.m. until 10:30 p.m. The funeral directors told me people were waiting for more than 2 ½ hours in line. It was the longest day of my life. I only had three cups of water during those 8 ½ hours and never left the receiving line. Family members were trying to get me to leave, but as long as people were in line and coming into the funeral home I wasn't going anywhere. Jeff's mother and Brian stayed right beside me for long periods. I was also told later that Al Hrabosky stood to my rear and kept a protective watch over me for several hours.

Thom Sehnert of Annie Gunn's had brought food for our family into the hospitality room, but I never saw the inside of the room. The funeral director told me later that one of their employees had a clicker to count the number of people filing through, and the total was close to 4,000. I know there were more who came and waited in line for more than an hour but who couldn't stay and had to leave before they got through the line. The director told me it was the biggest funeral in Bopp Chapel's more than 100 years in business. The Governor of Missouri, Bob Holden, came, as did some friends from

California, including Ronald Isley of the Isley Brothers, and many other great friends from all across the country, including my boyhood hero, Stan Musial.

The funeral was the next morning. Leading the procession from the Basilica to the cemetery were two fire trucks, about twenty police motorcycles, and another fifteen or so police squad cars. A television camera on a helicopter from Channel 2 showed the cars in the procession were backed up for more than two miles, bumper to bumper.

It was a great tribute to Jeff and everything he stood for. He was the kind of person who, when we would be out of town together, would see a stranger sitting on a park bench and ask him or her how they were doing. He enjoyed his life, he enjoyed every second of his life. Jim Koman was one of his best friends for more than twenty years and delivered one of the eulogies. Louis Birge said, "Jeff Clinton had more best friends than anybody I've ever known." Everybody he met wanted to be best friends with Jeff Clinton.

We had a reception at Schneithorst's, and when August Busch IV got back from New Orleans he came there and put his head in my shoulder and wept. He and Jeff had been very good friends. Two months later, when he found out that I wanted to take Jeff's boys to Disney World for a few days to get away from everything he set up a special trip for us to Discovery Cove where people can swim with the dolphins. It was amazing how healing it was for all of us, to be in the water swimming with the dolphins. It meant a lot to the boys and to all of us that we had a chance to be together in a different environment so we could forget about our tragedy, at least for a little while.

For forty days after Jeff was killed I wept at some point each day. I lost about twenty pounds, just for lack of appetite. All I was doing was going through the motions. I just had to keep forcing myself to get out of bed and keep going. Everything I was doing was almost just by reflex.

His mother Jo and I clung to each other pretty hard. We talked every day. Even though we had separated in 1983 and were divorced in 1989, no other person had ever come between us. We just developed different interests and grew apart, I know partially because I was so involved in my work. We remained friends, and she knows there is nothing in the world I wouldn't do for her, and I know the feeling is mutual. We shared a lot of great times in our life, and we also got through the worst time of our lives together.

It took me three months to acknowledge all the mass cards, flowers, charitable contributions and other expressions of sympathy. My secretary, Judy Cunetto, organized this effort and addressed the envelopes with a notation of their expression. I then wrote a personal note of appreciation—more than 2,000 of them. With each note I composed came the realization that my son was gone forever. With each admission of that fact it was like another nail had been driven into my heart.

My thoughts often came back to Jeff's two young boys, and to the last conversation I had with Jeff. On the day he was leaving for Homestead, I saw he had brought Nathan, the three-year-old, with him to the office. I said, "What's up? No preschool today?" Jeff told me that when he went to drop Nathan off at preschool he didn't want to go; he wanted to stay with his dad. He was very insistent, so Jeff said OK and brought him to the office.

Months later, Nathan told me, "I told my daddy he should not go to that race. I told him he would get killed if he went to that race." That was the day he wouldn't go to preschool and Jeff had brought him to the office. All I could imagine is that Nathan must have had a dream the night before. He really was clinging to his daddy that day. They are both very perceptive little boys, and I still often think back to that day.

My thoughts also kept turning to the crash. What had happened, and why? No matter if you are driving a racecar or just a personal car on the city streets you always try to minimize the risks you are taking and emphasize safety. You wear a seatbelt. You stop at intersections and look in both directions before you proceed. I was confident Jeff knew how to handle himself behind the wheel, and I knew he would not have deliberately stepped into a racecar that he didn't think was safe. For any professional racing team safety is paramount.

I have been critical of professional racing in the past because I don't think they take safety as importantly as they should. They have technical inspections and lengthy rules about the technology of the cars, but it seemed to me the governing bodies were always more concerned with somebody trying to cheat to get three or four additional horsepower than with checking all of the safety gear to make certain the driver was protected. I really think that was the situation in this case. I don't think that NASPORT, the governing body of the racing series, paid enough attention to safety.

I spent a lot of time trying to find out what happened. What I learned was that Jeff had run a couple of laps around the track at a slow speed, warming up the drive train and the tires. His car was a Budweiser Lola Nissan. It was a very windy day, as it often is in Florida, with gusts of up to thirty miles an hour. As Jeff went into the first turn going a little faster, a gust of wind caught the car just as a bump in the track lifted the front and flipped it up in the air. The car flipped and landed upside down. The roll bar snapped off and left Jeff totally exposed. That should not have been a fatal accident. Jeff should have been able to get out of the car and walk away. The roll bar should have protected him.

A few weeks later Mario Andretti was driving his son Michael's car at Indianapolis before Michael qualified for the Indy 500, and his car flipped over and slid probably 1,000 feet down the track. Mario got up and walked away. The roll bar did what it was supposed to do, protect the driver.

I realized immediately that something had to have been wrong with Jeff's car. I called my lawyer and told him we had to get possession of the car; that something had to have been wrong with it. He dispatched some people from his office, and we confiscated the car. We later ended up buying it.

When we had expert technicians inspect the car, we discovered that the roll bar had snapped off because it had not been properly secured on one side. You could not see that from outside the car. We learned that the designers had made a revision in the car, but the engineers had apparently not allowed for fueling considerations so the roll bar had to be moved. It should have been welded to the frame, but when they moved it, it was only riveted to the sheet metal tub that surrounded the driver. It was a basic engineering error in the design of the car which somebody should have found and fixed before any driver ever took that car out on the track.

We reconstructed the car and saw how the components had failed under impact. I don't see how anybody could have let the car go out on the track like that. It angers me and bewilders me, and I don't want to ever see another person being duped the way Jeff was into a false sense of security. He had equipment that was supposed to be state of the art, and it was far from that.

I also think there must be some flaws in the design of the Homestead racetrack. Four years later, in March 2006, another St. Louisian, Paul Dana, was killed in an accident at Homestead when he was warming up for a race. There has been a third fatal accident as well that I am aware of.

Everybody that knew Jeff and loved him was hurting so deeply. Jeff's friends donated most of his personal belongings to charity. They brought me a couple of his racing jackets. It took me about two months to get his Rolex watch back from the Dade County coroner's office. I had another Rolex watch in addition to a watch he had won in a racing series.

A few months after the accident I was talking with Ellie, Jeff's former wife, and she told me the boys had said they didn't have anything that had belonged to their dad. The boys were coming over for a sleepover, and I told her I would let them see the watches.

I will never forget asking Mark if he wanted to see his dad's watch. I took it out of the safe and watched as he sat on the floor and unwrapped it. His eyes were as big as saucers. He remembered the watch being on his daddy's wrist. I told him the watch was going home with him, and that his brother would get another Rolex watch, which I had given Jeff for his twenty-first birthday. He said very thoughtfully, "This will be very special to me."

I couldn't believe what I was hearing. Mark was five years old, and to have that kind of emotion and insight was astounding. I also took out the two racing jackets and gave them to the boys. Mark wrapped himself up in one jacket and laid down on the floor.

I didn't think the depth of sorrow could grow any deeper, but it did.

Thank God the boys have a wonderfully dedicated mother in Ellie Williams, who gives them great love and guidance in making this major adjustment in their lives.

One thought I could not get out of my mind was how a couple of years earlier, I suddenly had a great desire to buy cemetery plots for our family. I decided to get a mausoleum in Resurrection Cemetery in Shrewsbury. I wanted it made out of Missouri red granite, for obvious reasons. I went to an art glass company and had a special leaded window made. I had it designed with a golden challice as part of the Celtic cross in the center, and on the outside were three wavy lines representing the rivers around St. Louis and the fleur de lis representing St. Louis. It took about a year and a half to complete the project.

When it was done I took a picture and went to show it to Jeff. He said, "Dad, I don't want to look at that kind of thing."

As I reflected back on that and other moments, it seemed odd to me that I had been so driven to do that when nobody in our family was ill. Six months after it was finished I lost my son. It was almost eerie. I know I had done it just so my family wouldn't have to go through that process if something had happened to me, but I never dreamed I would be the one entombing my son.

Four years later, I still can't believe it.

Chapter 14

A FEW WEEKS AFTER JEFF's death, I was at home on a cold and rainy Sunday evening in late March. Terri Larkin had brought over some food she had prepared. I had not been eating well, and she was determined to see that I received some nourishment. Just as I was finishing dinner, the phone rang. It was Carole Buck, Jack's wife. Jack's health was rapidly deteriorating, and he had spent the last several months at Barnes-Jewish Hospital.

Carole said, "Jack wants to see you." I replied, "What day would be best?" She said, "No, he wants to see you tonight."

I explained that I had not shaved and was wearing a sweater and jeans, and she said, "Come as you are, there's nobody else here." As I drove to the hospital, I wondered how I was going to be able to greet my dear friend while being so consumed with my own grief.

When I reached Jack's floor, Carole was waiting at the elevator and warned me that his appearance had changed. He had lost a lot of weight, and his head had been shaved as a result of the brain operation that had stopped the body tremors, a symptom of his Parkinson's illness. Carole did not follow me to the corner room, allowing for our private meeting.

When the curtains were pulled back, I could see that the medical problems had taken their toll. Jack was very thin and weak, and the booming voice that had described Cardinal baseball games and other sports for decades had been reduced to a soft whisper.

Jack raised his hand and motioned for me to come to his bedside. He then formed the word "ice" with his mouth, and I asked the nurse for a cup of ice. After feeding him a couple of spoonfuls, he then softly said, "I want you to remember, Jeff died doing what he loved to do."

I replied, "I know, Jack, but the pain is still great." He said, "I know," then asked me to close my eyes. I closed them as I held his hand. We remained silent for several minutes. He was very tired, and I told him, "I have to go now Jack. I love you pal."

Carole later told me Jack was praying when he asked me to close my eyes. As I drove home in the rain, I kept thinking this wonderful man, who was in such pain and so near death, had the presence of mind to be concerned about my pain. Such a friend.

A few weeks later Jack died. I know he greeted Jeff for me when he got to Heaven. I was proud to be asked by his family to serve as an honorary pallbearer. Within a couple of months, I had lost my son and perhaps the best friend I could have.

Jack and I first met when we both were serving on the board of trustees of the Cystic Fibrosis Foundation. It was a natural association, since Jack was the Cardinals' announcer, the team was owned by Anheuser-Busch, and my company, Grey Eagle, was the Anheuser-Busch distributor for St. Louis County.

I never will forget the time that I went with Jack to Houston for a weekend series between the Cardinals and Houston Astros, and then we went on to Washington, where he was broadcasting a Monday night football game for CBS Radio. We got into a cab, and when Jack started talking, the driver whipped his head around and said, "Are you Jack Buck?" He had not recognized the face, but he knew Jack's voice.

At dinner that night, we met up with Hank Stram, the former coach who was Jack's football broadcasting partner. Jack wanted to have some fun with Hank, so he got me to pretend that I was helping the brewery select some new spokesmen for the Natural Light beer advertising campaign. The product was new and becoming very popular at the time. A lot of sports people, such as Nick Buoniconti, were involved as spokesmen in the ad campaign, and when I mentioned that Anheuser-Busch was looking for some new people, Hank's ears really perked up. Jack was kicking me under the table, telling me to keep laying it on.

Hank asked how much something like that would pay, and I said I thought it likely would be around $500,000 a year. Jack was trying so hard not to laugh I thought he was going to explode. Hank acted sincere in letting me know that he would be very interested in doing that kind of work. We finally let him know it was a joke.

We could only get one twin room in the hotel, so Jack and I were roommates for a night. I didn't know that he wore contact lenses, and when he took them out, he had reading glasses with lenses that were about as big as the bottom of a Coke bottle. He came out of the bathroom wearing them and scared the living heck out of me.

At 7:15 the next morning, I was sound asleep and suddenly I realized Jack was awake, doing interviews for the radio by telephone. He did five or six shows. I rolled over and said, "Jack, I am finished with you as a roomie. I need a quiet room to sleep. You make too much noise."

At the conclusion of the trip, I told him I thought because I had been traveling with the famous Jack Buck we would be eating in the fanciest restaurants with upfront tables and meeting a lot of famous people. Instead, one day we had lunch in the National Library basement cafeteria, because Jack had wanted to go to the Library and tour the Smithsonian.

We went to Ireland together. Also in our group were Mike and Lee Roarty; Stan and Lil Musial; Norm Crosby and his wife, Joanie; Gene and Jackie Autry, and some others. I took my sons, Jeff and Brian, and I kept trying to explain to them who Gene Autry was for most of the trip. They had never heard of Gene Autry.

I told them he was a post–World War II singing cowboy, along with Roy Rogers. They still didn't know who he was. One night we came out of our hotel room, and coming down the stairs, we saw Gene sitting at the piano. He was singing "Rudolph the Red-Nosed Reindeer."

"So that's who he is," both Jeff and Brian said. "Dad, how

come you never told us he was the guy who sang Rudolph?" I had never thought about it. I knew him as a cowboy.

Our group was over there for the Budweiser Irish Derby, the traditional horse race that Anheuser-Busch had just begun sponsoring. There were Budweiser signs and labels all around the track, but everything was decorated in a first-class manner. I remember standing at the rail next to two older Irish gentlemen. Listening, I heard one say to the other, "Well they certainly taught us what Budweiser is." His friend replied, "Yes, but they taught us some other things too. It is good to have them here."

Change is not always bad. Even an elder Irishman knew that.

Anytime you were around Jack, it was a fun and exciting time. After the death of another friend, Jack Carney, the popular host of the morning show on KMOX, Bob Hyland asked Jack to fill in as the host until a replacement could be found. Jack had been doing the show for about three months and he was running out of topics. He called me one day and asked me to be on his show the next morning.

"For what purpose, Jack?" I asked.

"I want you to do the Duke, to do your John Wayne impersonation," Jack said.

I enjoyed doing it but always thought it was pretty feeble. For some reason, every time Jack heard it he would fall down laughing. I told Jack I couldn't do it, and he said, "Why not?"

"Jack, I am supposed to be a fairly serious businessman in this community," I said. "I represent a consumer product, and I don't want to make a fool out of myself."

The dialogue went back and forth for several minutes, with Jack begging me to do it. I finally agreed, under the condition that he not identify me by my real name. I told him that when I went on the air, I was going to give him a fictitious name and that he had to accept it and go on. Jack agreed.

I knew what Jack was trying to do. He always did an impersonation of Clark Gable, and he wanted to get his wife,

Carole, on the air to do her Carol Channing impersonation. He said, "We'll have some fun."

At 9:05 the next morning, my phone rang and it was Jack's producer. He said Jack would be with me in one minute, and for that entire sixty seconds all I could think of was, "How am I going to pull this off?"

Jack came on the air and said, "This morning we are going to have people give us their favorite impersonations. We have a caller on the line right now," and he came to me.

He asked who he was talking to, and I launched into my John Wayne impersonation, "Well, what do you mean who is this." Jack was already laughing. "Folks, it's the Duke," he said.

"Pilgrim, what's your name?" I asked.

When he answered "Jack Buck," I said, "Buck? I once had a horse named Buck. We had to put the critter down." Jack asked what the problem was with the horse, and I said, "I had him gelded, and he developed a new gate and it gave me saddle sores."

Jack was laughing like crazy. We went on for about ten minutes. He asked me what I was doing now, and I said, "I'm running a little school teaching boys how to be cowboys." Jack asked how I did that. "We take them out on the range and I tell them you have to ride hard and do everything I tell you to do, and when you get back to the bunk house at night it's very important to remember to keep your hands off the other fellers' equipment." Jack was laughing uncontrollably.

Finally he said, "This has been Duke Wayne. Who are we really talking to?"

I said, "This is Wilber Pinkley of Warren County." Jack called me later and said he had been rolling on the floor. I told him, "See ya' later Pilgrim" and went off to work.

Much like with Jack, it is always easy to have a good time when you are in the company of Dan Dierdorf. After Jeff died, Dan was also there constantly offering his support and friendship, and I will forever be grateful to him.

Somewhat surprisingly, I think we met in a bar back in

the early 1970s. A lot of the old football Cardinals were in the Sportsman's Lounge off Highway 40 one night when I happened to be there, and I sent them over some cold pitchers of Budweiser. They thanked me, and I explained I was the local Budweiser distributor. We struck up a friendship.

Steve Jones, a running back on the Cardinals, was the one who had come over to thank me. I ended up hiring Steve when a neck injury ended his playing career. He has been with Grey Eagle for more than twenty-five years. I often tell Steve, "One of the best runs you ever made was from the table to the bar where I was sitting."

Dan was a big boxing fan, and later he announced pro boxing matches. I took him to the Golden Gloves and we went to the Fox Theater to watch the closed circuit coverage of the Roberto Duran–Sugar Ray Leonard fight. Jim Hanifan was with us too. Being a beer salesman, I fit right in with that crowd.

When Dan's playing career was over, he suggested we put together a slow-pitch softball team. I provided the uniforms. We called our team the "Busch Bisons."

One day Dan suggested we take the team over to Grant's Farm and get a photo taken with one of the buffalo there. I thought it was a great idea and said I would provide my motor coach so we all could go together. We set it up with the farm manager and they let us come onto the property. We saw a buffalo, stopped, and got out of the motor coach.

Dan and I started to walk up to where the buffalo was grazing, and it bolted. As I recall, it ran toward the other buffalo and started a stampede. It was just like you see in the movies. I looked at Dan, and he was looking at me out of the corner of his eye. "Whatever made us think we could come out here and take our picture with a buffalo?" he said. "I have no idea," I replied, "but I went along with it."

We got back to the bus safely, and stopped off at the Barnhoff area. Cletus, the manager, said he had a solution for us. There was a buffalo head hanging in the carriage house, and he took it off the wall and carried it outside. We all huddled around it and put one horn on Terry Stieve's shoulder and the other horn on Dan's shoulder. The buffalo looked as if it was standing right among us. That was our team photo.

We didn't win many games but we always had a good time. We had the motor coach there and we never ran out of cold Budweiser.

Another great friend I enjoyed knowing was John Krey III. John was from the meatpacking business and was a boyhood friend of August Busch III. Later in life, I met John after he bought the Anheuser-Busch distributorship for St. Charles and St. Peters, Missouri, from the late Harold Sherer. John was a large man with sandy-colored hair and a friendly face, and he smiled often. He was a great outdoor sportsman, and I learned later he was of superior intelligence and perhaps one of the best big-game hunters in the world.

John used to invite me to the Wings of St. Albans in west St. Louis County for duck and pheasant shooting. We would shoot pen-raised ducks in the morning from blinds located in line of a pond, their fly-way destination. After lunch and good fellowship discussion, we would head to the fields for afternoon pheasant shooting.

After several shooting experiences with John, he asked me to join himself and a group of friends on an upcoming "wing shooting" trip to Denmark. The group included Hord and Bunny Armstrong, the Ted Bakewells, Orrin "Sage" Wightman, and August Busch III, among others.

My response was, "John, I can't do it. I can't shoot with these people; they have belonged to gun clubs all their lives. I don't want to make a fool of myself." John said, "Jerry, I have stood behind your blind at St. Albans and watched you knock down doubles (shooting with two shells in a gun, knocking down one bird with each shell). You can shoot with anybody. Besides, you will fly in first class with me. Some of these folks don't like to fly up front." (John's size dictated a wider seat that first-class offers.) I just laughed and said, "OK, John, let's do it."

It was October 1986, and we flew to Copenhagen, then on to Odeuse to the island of Fyn. Our home for the trip was Falsled

Kro, perhaps the finest country inn in Denmark. Our first shoot was for pheasant, and took place at the historic Barritskov Estate in Jettland. We arrived at an open area in the rolling terrain, and it was decided that we would have two lines of shooters. The novice guns—me—would be on the front line, and the more experienced guns—John, August, and most of the rest—would be on the back line. The theory was that if the novice line missed, the back line would bring down the birds.

The shoot began. I was stationed at the bottom of a descending hill with the "beaters" above on the flat field moving toward me. Suddenly, a pheasant was flushed out and began to fly in my direction. It seemed with every foot he flew in my direction he gained two feet in altitude. There was nothing I could do. This first bird of the hunt was going to fly right over my head—it was my bird. I threw the gun up to my shoulder and pointed it skyward. The bird was gaining altitude fast.

I led the pheasant by about four feet and pulled the trigger. The bird collapsed its wings and dropped from the sky like a missile. It sailed over my head and landed at the feet of August Busch III. August looked stunned as he lifted his head and shouted at me, "Clinton, where the hell did you learn to shoot like that?"

"The housing project, August," I said, "the housing project."

Needless to say we all had a great laugh to begin the hunt, and nobody laughed harder than John Krey.

On the last evening of the hunt, it was suggested that each member stand at his place at the table and offer their own remarks about the hunt. When it was my turn, I said I was very grateful to John for introducing me to wing shooting and I was especially grateful for him teaching me that for 85 percent more I could go first class.

That was our last hunt together. A few months after returning home, John Krey III died of a very aggressive cancer. I miss his good fellowship.

Of all the things I have experienced in my life, I know I am the most grateful for the love of family and friends.

Chapter 15

WITHOUT JEFF, EVERYTHING IN MY life changed. I was already getting tired of the beer business because there had been so many changes in the industry over the past several years, and I really lost my enthusiasm and desire to be involved any longer. It was not a fun business anymore, and without Jeff it left me drained.

It would have been a much smoother transition to turn the company over to Jeff, but with that no longer a possibility, I made the decision to sell Grey Eagle in 2005 to David Stokes, an executive at Anheuser-Busch. He also is the oldest son of Patrick Stokes, at the time the president and chief operating officer of Anheuser-Busch Companies, Inc.

I wanted to reinvigorate myself and get away from the business and put all of those years behind me. I didn't want to live it day in and day out anymore, negotiating contracts and dealing with industry issues and all of the operational problems that come up. It was not interesting to me anymore. I guess the challenge was gone.

It would have certainly been a smoother exodus and transition had Jeff been alive to take over the company, because then I know it would have felt more comfortable for me to come back and visit and still be involved in some of the company activities. That possibility feels out of place for me now, and I don't think I have the liberty to do that under present circumstances.

Still, I was glad I made the decision because I knew I was at the point where I needed to start another chapter in my life.

I have always thought that the entrepreneur was the backbone of our society, those individuals who are willing to take risks and think on their feet. There is more involved in running a successful business than taking a blueprint from a manufacturer and simply following the dotted line. I didn't believe in operating that kind of business. I believed in running a business where you had to be on your feet and alert and creative, with a plan to go forward and make your business bigger and better. Unfortunately, I believe the opposite of that is becoming more prevalent in the industry today.

I don't want this to come off as a case of sour grapes. I have had an unbelievable life and accomplished far more than I ever would have dreamed, all because of Anheuser-Busch and Grey Eagle. I spent 42 ½ years at Grey Eagle and 7 years before that at Anheuser-Busch, virtually all of my adult working life. I was the last original Grey Eagle employee still working for the company at the time I sold the business.

What both Anheuser-Busch and Grey Eagle did was to allow me to be challenged. I always believed that if you are not challenged, then you can't realize your potential. I don't know many people who work at 100 percent of their potential, but that is always a goal to strive for. Nobody knows 100 percent of their potential until they are challenged to see if they can do more than they have ever done.

I always enjoyed that aspect of the beer business. It has been challenging over the years, and I think it gave me the opportunity to look for other challenges in my life. Accepting the challenge was the reason I started driving a racecar, the reason I worked so hard to get a domed stadium built, and to try to bring an NFL team back to St. Louis. It was the reason I always tried to sell more beer than my competitors. It was the reason I worked so hard to raise money for charitable causes. Those were all challenges that drove my career.

I probably obtained more for myself by accepting the challenges over the years, coming to grips with it, and dealing with it than by doing a job that required only using the same skills day in and day out.

My life really started to change the day Tom Burrows presented me with a challenge of preparing a sales budget for Grey Eagle during the early years of the company, an event described earlier in this book. Tom Burrows had a great deal of confidence in me, and I know he saw more potential in me than I saw in myself. He told me on very short notice to prepare a sales budget. I accepted that challenge and stayed up all night creating the budget. When I went into the meeting the next day, I knew what I was talking about and what all of the numbers meant.

Once I had done that, I had the confidence that I could do it because I knew the mechanics of how to do it. Accepting that challenge gave me a new confidence, and I knew that if I would continue to accept the challenges as they came along I could go far in my career.

Like anybody who reaches this point in their life, I know there are things I wish had been different, but I don't know if that would have been possible. I know I left my first wife, Jo, home alone too much. She realized what the beer business was like, and how much time it took, when her son Jeff started adapting the same hours and lifestyle I had been living for years. It was not uncommon for me to work all day, leave the office to coach a Little League game, then go back to the office to finish up the day's work and get home and have my dinner around 11 p.m. That wasn't fair to Jo, and I know it, but the beer business takes that kind of dedication to be successful. You have to work nights and weekends, whatever it takes. That was a decision I made, and it made those sacrifices bearable for me.

I was involved in everything I thought was fun and worthwhile. I believe for anyone to enjoy their job it has to be fun. When I decided that I no longer enjoyed it, then I made a change in my life.

Looking back on all of the wonderful friendships I have made and maintained over the years, I realize how lucky I have been. It has been my honor to be friends with people such as Jack Buck, Dan Dierdorf, and all of the other football Cardinals like Jackie Smith, Jim Hart, Conrad Dobler, Roger Wehrli, Johnny Roland, and so many more. People from the baseball world such as Stan Musial, Whitey Herzog, and Al Hrabosky became good friends.

I was part owner of the Blues and the Steamers, which helped produce more friendships and gave me a good feeling because I thought we were doing something worthwhile, giving back to the community by helping keep those sports businesses in operation.

I have many friends from the political world, both Republicans and Democrats. I don't want to begin to list them all because I would invariably leave somebody out, and I would hear from them about it later.

I don't know what challenges lie ahead for me. I know I want to stay involved with my five grandsons—Mark and Nathan (Jeff and Ellie's boys), and Riley, Myles, and Cole (Brian and Megan's children). I want to see them develop with the proper education and grow up with the proper values, ready to be productive citizens. I have some years left in me and think I have the ability to assist their parents to do that. That's my legacy. Doing that and working with the charities that interest me will keep me busy and provide fulfillment.

I think it is important to have a reason to get out of bed in the morning and go somewhere. I have that, even if it is to just check the stock reports and see how my investments are doing. I'm fortunate in that I always seem to have a lot going on and something to do, or some place where I need to be. I am never bored.

I don't know what my next challenge is going to be, or what the next challenge facing our society will be. I have been witness to a great deal of change over the years, and I really don't think President Kennedy ever got enough credit when he pledged that the United States would put a man on the moon during the decade of the 1960s. It was a challenge he gave to the country, and the men and women of the space program were able to meet that challenge.

A lot of things in our life have changed because of the space program, with the development of the computer chip. Have you ever thought what would happen if somebody said they were going to take our cell phones away and get rid of satellite television? People would think we were back living in the Stone Age.

What did we do before we had computers? We stayed up all night pounding a calculator. It is a staggering change.

I remember growing up as a young boy, we didn't have electricity in our house. We had coal oil lamps with a wick in them. I remember we got a new type of lamp that operated under pressure and projected a much greater range of light. We thought it was really something.

Now we have cars that tell us if we make a wrong turn when we are trying to reach our destination. It is really kind of hard to believe when you think about it.

What will our challenges be in the future, both collectively and individually? I can't wait to find out.

Appendix

JERRY G. CLINTON WAS THE Chairman of the Board and Chief Executive Officer of Grey Eagle Distributors, Inc., the St. Louis County wholesaler of Anheuser-Busch products from 1980 until he sold the company in 2005.

Clinton successfully worked with state and local elected officials to make the St. Louis domed stadium a reality and to return the National Football League to St. Louis.

Clinton, through Grey Eagle and personal gifts, provides financial support to hundreds of philanthropic organizations in the St. Louis area each year. He has chaired or co-chaired numerous fundraising events on behalf of local charities.

Clinton served on the board of directors of several organizations, including the St. Louis Ambassadors and the Gateway Chapter of the Cystic Fibrosis Foundation. He is one of the three founders of the Civic Entrepreneurs Organization, a group whose goal is to promote the metropolitan St. Louis area.

He founded the Jerry Clinton LPGA Pro-Am Golf Tournament, which raised more than $1 million to fight cancer. He chaired a successful $400,000 capital fundraising campaign for Marygrove, a Florissant residential treatment center for adolescents, and he was named Marygrove's "Man of the Year" in 1988.

A former Golden Gloves and AAU champion, he sponsors the annual Golden Gloves tournament in St. Louis. He also created and sponsored the Budweiser Guns and Hoses night that features bouts between area police officers and firefighters, raising more than $1.6 million for the St. Louis-area Backstoppers, an organization that supports the families of police officers or firefighters who have lost their lives in the line of duty.

In addition to his NFL efforts, Clinton's ties to professional sports are numerous. He has been instrumental in keeping national professional sports in St. Louis by ownership positions in the St. Louis Blues of the National Hockey League and the St. Louis Steamers of the Major Indoor Soccer League.

Clinton's contributions to the St. Louis region have been recognized by key organizations, including:

- ✓ • In 2005, a section of 7th Street at Convention Plaza in St. Louis was named "Jerry Clinton Way" by the St. Louis Board of Aldermen in recognition of Clinton's leading role in the construction of the domed stadium.
- • Honored in 2005 by the Asthma & Allergy Foundation of America for serving four years as chairman of the annual fundraising gala.
- ✓ • Received the "Heart of the Community" Award from the Mary Ryder Home in 2004.
- • Was awarded the 2004 Missourian Award for the American Heart Association, Heartland affiliate.
- • In 2004, received the Jack Buck Award from the Missouri Athletic Club.
- • Was presented the "Champion for Kids" Award from the St. Louis Variety Club in 2004.
- • Received Marianist Retreat and Conference Center Youth Medal in 2003.
- • Received the Mayor James Eagan Award from Marygrove in 2003.
- • Was inducted into the St. Louis Gateway Classic Sports Foundation/St. Louis Recreation Boxing Hall of Fame in 2003.
- • In 2003, was presented the Dr. Robert Hyland/Rick Hummel Award for Meritorious Service to Sports

by the St. Louis Chapter of the Baseball Writers Association of America.

- Was made a Missouri Honorary Police Chief by the Missouri Police Chiefs Association in 2002.
- Inducted into the Missouri Sports Hall of Fame in Springfield as a member of the Class of 2002.
- In 1997, received the AMC Cancer Research Center "Crystal" Award for charitable leadership.
- Was the winner of the 1995 St. Louis · Argus Distinguished Citizen Award.
- Received the Spirit of St. Louis Award from the Multiple Sclerosis Society in 1994.
- Was named the Ambassador of the Year by the St. Louis Ambassadors in 1989.
- Was selected "Man of the Year" by the St. Louis Construction Trades Council in 1985.
- The combined St. Louis County Chambers of Commerce awarded him the "Businessman of the Year" Award in 1985.
- Received the Meritorious Service to Sports Award from the St. Louis Multiple Sclerosis Society in 1983.
- Was named "Sportsman of the Year" by the St. Louis Ambassadors in 1983.

Clinton was one of Grey Eagle's original employees when the company was founded in 1963. He rose from truck dispatcher through sales and marketing positions to become president of the company in 1976 at the age of thirty-nine. He acquired full ownership and became chairman in 1980.

Under Clinton's leadership, the company's market share increased to an unprecedented 77 percent for package beer and more than 90 percent for draught beer. Grey Eagle is the largest independent beer distributor in the Midwest and one of the largest in the country operating from one location.

Clinton's commitment to quality has resulted in numerous

industry awards and recognition for the company. Grey Eagle received the prestigious "Ambassador" recognition for twelve consecutive years when the program was implemented by Anheuser-Busch in 1982 to recognize its top wholesalers for excellence in all phases of operations for community and civic involvement.

Grey Eagle has been a leader of efforts to prevent alcohol abuse and drunk driving. "None for the Road," an educational campaign and the first of its type, was launched by Grey Eagle in 1982 and has been a model for similar programs across the country.

Clinton served two years as Chairman of the Missouri Beer Wholesalers Association.

In 1993, Clinton retired as a driver from automotive racing in the Sports Car Club of America's professional Trans-Am Series. The Trans-Am Series races are held throughout the United States, Canada, and Mexico.

He was the "Rookie of the Year" in the St. Louis Region of the SCCA in 1983. He won the GT-4 championship in the club's Midwest division in 1984 and was the Midwest's GT-1 champion in 1985. Also that year, he was the winner of the Ford National Cup, given annually to the nation's top GT-1 driver of a Ford-powered car.

In 2004, Clear Channel Communications featured six people in the St. Louis community in a 30-minute program titled, "Visionaries." Clinton's segment was entered in Emmy judging for the category "Interviews/Discussion" and won the Emmy.

A native St. Louisian, Clinton graduated in 1955 from Hadley Technical High School, where he received specialized training in commercial art. He studied sales and marketing at the University College of Washington University.

Upon his retirement in 2005, Clinton received the Lifetime Achievement Award from the National Beer Wholesalers Association.